New Wineskins for

New Wine

Turning followers of Jesus into Over Comers

Robert Farrier

Published by CreateSpace

Unless otherwise indicated, all Scripture quotations are from *The Holy Bible, New King James Version* © Copyright 1982

Scripture quotations noted NLT are taken from The New Living Translation, © Copyright 1996. All rights reserved. Used by permission.

Scripture quotations noted NCV are taken from The Holy Bible, New Century Version © Copyright 2005 by Thomas Nelson, Inc. Used by permission.

ISBN-13: 978-1500225322
ISBN-10: 1500225320

For additional copies, you can order from
Publisher or online at Amazon.com

Reference: 1. Inspirational 2. Culture and Worldviews
3. Kingdom Living

This book was previously published under the title, Created by God, BORN TO RULE, by STM Publication

ISBN-13-978-09789842-6-7
ISBN-10-0978984269

Contents

Chapter One

The End of Freedom

We have reached a time and place in history when the Church must awaken to the reality of what has been written in Scripture concerning the future of the earth. There has been many false prophets that have predicted the "end" and they have been found wanting. These false prophets remind us of the shepherd boy, who, when watching over a flock of sheep, brought out the villagers three or four times by crying out, "Wolf! Wolf!" When his neighbors came to help him, he laughed at them for their trouble.

Then the Wolf really did come; the Shepherd boy, now truly frightened, cried out in terror, "Pray, do come and help me; the Wolf is killing the sheep"; but no one paid any heed to his cries, nor rendered any assistance. The Wolf, having no cause of fear, unhurriedly destroyed the whole flock.

Here is the warning for us today

Many are predicting the downfall of America. This warning is coming, not only from the teachers of biblical prophecy but also from worldly students of philosophy and economics. Can there be any truth in their warnings? I believe there is. We, however, are not crying 'wolf' to put fear into your heart but to prepare you for what is to come. The times of the end are here, so let us not be caught off guard like the villagers in this story when the wolf really came. We must be prepared.

The end started centuries ago when 'Cain' set up the first 'State' government. Since then his followers have brought forth Utopian ideas that strip every individual of his identity and make him subordinate to the state. The Elite have decided that each person's first duty must be to the state – not to family, community or to his faith. The individual must not own anything that will challenge the authority of the state.

Whatever schemes have been contrived in the past, they have always come from a heart that desires to have power over others. They have clothed it in terms that have deceived the people, leading them to believe that they have their best interests at heart.

The methods used to transform a society into the dreams of the intellectuals (those who claim to be wise) have not changed from the beginning of time. We see them used repeatedly and now we see them being used in America and elsewhere.

These methods (1) destroy the moral fabric of a society (2) undermine the family (3) destroy the economy and the value of their currency (4) belittle patriotism and a national sense of purpose and (5) control the media to promote their agenda.

The people who desire power to control others will always find a receptive audience among the disenchanted, dissatisfied and those who are not willing to accept responsibility or blame for their condition in life. They are lured by false hope, built on false promises, to believe that if they follow their new leader, he/she will lead them to equality with those who have worked hard, sacrificed much and took risks to achieve their success.

NOW is the time when the church must get itself prepared to confront the final attack that it will encounter. That which is fast approaching will affect every race on every continent. It will affect the rich and the poor, the educated and the illiterate, and the powerful as well as the weak. It will affect the Christian and non-Christian alike. That which is coming will bring monumental change to all people everywhere.

What's Up?

In Rio de Janeiro, Brazil (1992), the UN passed 'UN Agenda 21/Sustainable Development'. This resolution has had the backing of ALL the governments of the World and the backing of Presidents Bush (1and 2) Clinton and Obama. It has, however never been brought forth to the US congress. This 351-page document is the blue print for a One World Government. This is not a conspiracy theory; this is a fact.

In 1996, the Earth Charter Commission, co-chaired by Russia's Mikhail Gorbachev and Canada's, Maurice Strong, was formed to over-see the drafting process of the new Earth Charter. The final text was agreed upon in March 2000 in Paris and was officially lunched at the Peace Palace in The Hague on June 29, 2000. The original copy of the Earth Charter has been placeed in a specially constructed ARK OF HOPE, a wooden chest built to resemble the Biblical Ark of the Covenant.

The Earth Charter states we must recognize that we are one human family and a one Earth Community with a common destiny. As they see it, we must join together to bring about a sustainable global society founded on: 1) respect for nature 2) universal rights 3) economic justice and 4) a culture of peace.

It says we must (A) preserve: 1) a healthy biosphere with all its ecological systems (i.e., go Green). 2) a rich variety of plants and animals (i.e. save the whale, etc) 3) fertile soils, pure water and clean air (i.e. stop oil exploration and coal burning). (B) We must eliminate: 1) Injustice, poverty, ignorance and violent conflict (i.e. establish international law, spread the wealth, take over the school system and have a UN military for the world). (C) We must form a global partnership. Fundamental changes are needed in Values, Institutions and Ways of living, as our environmental, economic, political, social and spiritual challenges are interconnected (i.e. we must be TOLERANT of each other). (D) We must decide to live with a universal responsibility, identifying ourselves with the whole earth community (i.e. lose our national sovereignty).

The Earth Charter goes on to enumerate 16 Principles that the World's governments must abide by. Here are a few unchanged quotes from The Earth Charter (emphasis mine):

1) Affirm that with increased freedom, knowledge and power comes increased responsibility to promote the *common good*.

2) Promote *social and economic justice*, enabling all to achieve a secure and meaningful livelihood that is ecologically responsible.

3) *Manage the extraction* and use of non-renewable resources such as minerals and fossil fuels in ways that minimize depletion and cause serious environmental change.

4) Ensure that decision-making addresses the *cumulative long tern, indirect long-distance and global consequences of human activities.*

5) *Avoid military activities* damaging the environment.

6) Act with restraint and efficiency when using energy and *rely increasingly on renewable energy sources such as solar and wind.*

7) *Ensure universal access to health care* that fosters reproductive health and responsible reproduction.

8) Empower every human being with the education and resources to secure a sustainable livelihood and *provide social society and safety nets* for those who are unable to support themselves.

9) Promote the *equitable distribution of wealth within nations and among nations.*

10) Ensure that *all trade supports sustainable resources use, environmental protection and progressive labor standards.*

11) Honor and support the young people of our communities, enabling them to *fulfill their essential role in creating sustainable societies.*

12) Promote *the contribution of the arts and humanities* as well as the

sciences in sustainability education.

13) *Enhance the role of the media* in raising awareness of ecological and social changes.

14) *Demilitarize national security systems* to the level of a non-provocative defense posture and military resources to peaceful purposes, including ecological restoration

In Summary, **The Earth Charter** states, "In order to build a sustainable global community, the nations of the world must renew their commitment to the United Nations, fulfilling their obligations under existing international agreements, and support the implementation of Earth Charter principles with an international legal binding instrument on environment and development".

In America, while its citizens were asleep, the powers that be, silently put into operation, by executive order and by regulation, the very tenets of The Earth Charter. By doing so, it by-passed its duly elected Congress and gave the power of implementation to hired political men and women.

May I state again, the present and past Presidents since 1992 have signed off on these principles. This is not something for the future; IT IS NOW! The time is coming when it will be introduced as a Bill in Congress to be signed into law, then what?

Every State, county, city in the United States has already implemented strategies into their plans to carry out The Earth Charter. Worldwide plans are already made and are now being carried out to tie the economies, security and the well-being of the world's nations together so that if one nation fails they all fail.

Why is this so important to us here in America and around the world? To the 'wise men' of this world, the only prevention of a catastrophe that will end this world *is the creation of a New World Order that has global governance.*

Who is behind all this upheaval?

We might think that it is a man or a group of men that are parlaying their influence and money to create this New World Order. There are indeed powerful men who have such dreams, but without their knowing it, they are mere pawns being played by the one who has more at stake in this game. His name is Satan. However, to Satan it is not a game because what is at stake is his kingdom. To rule the entire earth is his goal. This is his agenda. The only thing stopping him is the Church.

Those in power today would have the entire world to believe that this is just some kind of nonsense, some imaginary make-believe fantasy. However, Mankind has always believed in unseen creatures populating the aerial spaces. The thought of angels and devils that have come down and touched humanity is universal. Books have been written, images drawn and tales passed on from generation to generation about creatures from another realm.

This other realm is the spiritual realm and is just as factual as the natural realm we live in. We cannot see it with our physical eyes, but it is real nevertheless.

Among young people today the most popular books, movies, and TV shows almost all deal with the supernatural. It is on the minds of people inside and outside the Church. They have a desire to 'look into this other realm' because all they see coming where they 'live' is chaos and sorrow and pain. Young people today are without hope for a future that gives them promise.

Satan knows that whoever rules the kingdom, rules something more valuable than property and things. Whoever rules the kingdom, rules the hearts of men and receives WORSHIP from those who are subjects of the kingdom. This is his ultimate goal but God, the creator of all things, physical and Spiritual has other plans. God's Grand Plan is for His disciples to rule and reign with His Messiah, Jesus Christ over this earth. Therefore, this great spiritual war is between the Kingdom of God and Satan's kingdom of Darkness.

The heart of any kingdom is its culture; therefore, the battleground is the culture of the kingdom. Whoever wears the crown of KING gets to controls the culture.

The Kingdom Culture that God instilled into Adam and Eve was the first target of Satan after their expulsion from the Garden of Eden. The family of Adam and Eve soon found themselves in kingdom warfare within their family. Cain murdered his brother Abel, and then left to form the first humanistic family of the world. Man then found himself under the first state government, where men were ruling over men instead of God ruling over men. Cain's family developed its own culture and the war continued.

While Satan has been leading humanity onward to the final Battle of Armageddon (where all the nations will come against Israel), thinking that this will bring about his great overthrow of God's Kingdom, Jesus Christ quietly announced that a New World Order has already come. Jesus made the announcement, *"Repent, for the kingdom of*

Heaven is at hand."

This announcement is the fulfillment of the promise given to Adam and Eve. It proclaimed that at the conclusion of the ages, all kingdoms of the earth will come under the governmental authority of Jesus Christ and He will rule in Righteousness as King of kings and Lord of lords.

Leading up to this final battle, a number of dramatic events will be experienced in the earth. Many of these events are now being witnessed, such as changes in nature (increase in number of earthquakes, tornados and changes in weather patterns (drought and flooding), famine, increase in violence, wide spread sickness and disease. However, two of the biggest changes, the maneuvering of political powers around the world to bring about a one-world government and the attack on the cultures of the world but especially the attack on American culture are going unnoticed.

The second is so important because America is the last stronghold of a culture that is closest to the Kingdom Culture of the 1st and 2nd Century as displayed by the followers of Jesus Christ. Satan has succeeded in destroying faith in Christ throughout most of the world. There are pockets of Christ's followers but the most influential is found in the culture of the USA.

The culture of America is based on the Constitution that recognizes that their Creator endows its citizens with certain unalienable rights. Its laws are based on Biblical tradition. Two other aspects of its strength has been (1) the family unit that has been the cornerstone of the fabric of its society and (2) the majority of its citizens have had, until recently, knowledge of the Bible. Because of this God has prospered this nation.

All this has now changed; God's favor has been lifted from this nation. With two major proclamations by those in power, all hell is breaking loose on the USA. The first is the unleashing of the bonds of homosexuality and the acceptance of same -sex marriages. The second is our government's defiance against God's judgment and its assault on the Bible as a standard for righteousness and justice.

Jesus said, *"I will build my Church and the gates of hell will not prevail against it."* Therefore, it is up to His Church to fight the attack of this unseen supernatural force with the Supernatural force of God. The Church is still to extend His Kingdom throughout the world, making known this mystery by the power of the Holy Spirit.

It is the responsibility of the Church to preach the Gospel of the Kingdom of God; not to preach only, however, but to live it out in their daily lives. This living out is expressed in the culture of the Kingdom by those who are called disciples.

The battle is for the minds of men because it is in the mind that decisions are made as to how a person will live their life. It is in the mind, that people make judgments about what they accept into their spirit; which in turn affects who will be their master and whom they will worship.

A Time for Preparation

God has ordained a time for His church when He could touch her life. This touch would result in His glory being revealed in and through her in a greater way than ever before.

The time that God has ordained for His Church to make herself ready to be a dwelling place for Him, is NOW. God is moving in the hearts of leaders to raise up a people who are not content to be just followers of Jesus; people who have accepted no responsibility and who run from accountability. He is raising up leaders who are calling for men and women to be true disciples, drawing upon Jesus for their very life.

God is raising up His Apostles and Prophets who have a vision of the glory of a house that will be the dwelling place for the Lord and be the temple for the Holy Spirit. It is not the glory of the building that is their focus but that Christ will be glorified through the lives that He rules over as their king.

Those who are truly called to fulfill their function will not only live a life above reproach but also have a heart burdened to accomplish the Lord's command; make disciples that are matured and that have come into Sonship, worthy to be His bride and reign with Him.

Those who are not either Apostles or Prophets must also grasp the Lord's heart and cry out for the Lord of the harvest to raise up laborers, made ready for the coming harvest. These laborers will do more than just fast and pray for revival (which is local) but will cry out for a restoration of Kingdom Living. These Disciples will first give themselves to God, allowing Him to touch their lives in such a way that He may transform them into the very image of Jesus Christ. These will be the 21st century Disciples.

These 21st century disciples will submit to the will and dealings of their King in order to be willing vessels, filled with His life, power and glory. They will be filled with the Spirit of the Living God. These 21st

11

century disciples will experience the glory of the ministry of the Holy Spirit. The glory of His ministry will be more glorious than anything that we have read about regarding Moses, Solomon's temple, Peter or Paul or the great men and women of God in the last 150 years.

These 21st century disciples will be willing to learn what it means to sell all in order to buy the gold purified in the fire and will do all that is required in order to be clothed with white garments ready to meet their King. Unlike 'followers', 21st century disciples are disciplined in their thoughts and actions. They are faithful and devoted in their loyalty to their king.

Those who are content to be only 'followers' of Jesus, even though they may be doing what they think is 'kingdom work', will not be ready nor equipped to face the pending chaos and horrendous trouble that is coming upon the earth.

This book was written to prepare you to be a dwelling place for God's Spirit that you may bring Him glory and give you a vision of what God has planned for His people. It will provide you a track to run on in order for you to be the disciple that you desire to be by developing a deeper relationship with Christ your King and learning to be led by the Holy Spirit- maturing you into a position of Sonship.

The world and even the church views, 'rule and reign', as terms that convey control, regulate, dominate and supremacy. These words are void of mercy, compassion and understanding. However, in the context that they are used in this book and in the Bible, we see the love of God reaching out to His people that He might bless them and lead them to an abundant life. This abundant life is full of purpose and fulfillment.

As you continue to apply the following truths, you will be transformed into a disciple and then into an OverComer. You will find yourself on a fastback that jumpstarts you into supernatural living, Kingdom Living.

Chapter Two

Being Confortable with the Supernatural

Becoming an OverComer

If we are going to be a disciple of Jesus Christ and walk with Him, we must feel 'at home' with the supernatural. It should be as natural to us as breathing; for it is the very nature of the one who lives within us. It must not frighten us; we must feel relaxed in its presence in order to feel relaxed in His presence.

Young people today are looking for challenges that command their commitment and will rally their enthusiasm. Most of all, they are longing for a cause that is critical enough to demand their time. Most of all, they are looking for the supernatural.

Jesus came on the scene 2000 years ago to offer what young people were searching. He is still offering the same challenge today. He is not looking for followers that will sit on the sidelines but will join with him in the quest of extending His kingdom. He is offering, along with the challenges, a new way of living. He is offering them, Kingdom Life, a life in the supernatural. To live this life one must take that first vital step out of the natural into the supernatural.

It is a life full of battles but it is ultimately an overcoming life. It is to the OverComer that Jesus, our Savior King, presents the greatest rewards. The one who says He is the first and the last, who was dead and is now alive for evermore makes these promises to the OverComer:

- You shall eat of the Tree of Life that is in the midst of the paradise of God
- You shall not be hurt by the second death
- You shall receive some of the hidden manna, a white stone whereon is written a new name
- You shall receive power over the nations
- You will be clothed in white garments and your name, He will not blot out from the Book of Life
- You will be made a pillar in the temple of His God (the Father)
- You will be granted to sit with Him on His throne as He overcame and sat down with His Father

How might we describe an OverComer? We could start first by saying that he is a disciple, one who not only accepts the teachings of Jesus but has fallen in love with Him and willingly does the will of the Father. We could go on to use words that make known what he/she does like: Conquer, Defeat, Triumph-Over, Dominate, Vanquish, Occupy, and Take Control. These words describe the activity that God has called His Church to do.

Before you think that this challenge is for young people only, let me ask you to think again. Jesus calls out to all (no matter their age, sex, race, social-economic status) to come and join him.

God has placed His Church in a spiritually dark world and it is our assignment to overcome or conquer the darkness. There has never been a time when the forces of evil are coming together to destroy the peoples of the God as they are today. The wicked are using all the deceitful tactics of the evil One to drown out the voice of righteousness throughout the world.

There is a war to fight with many battles ahead for the OverComer. The Promise is given; the dream is ready to be planted in the heart of the OverComer. This book is written with the hope that God's people will be filled with faith and committed to go forth in obedience to the commands of their King.

Dull of Hearing

The Church of the Lord Jesus Christ has been infiltrated by compromise and humanism and is no longer the voice of God heralding the words of Christ, *"Repent for the Kingdom of God is at hand."*

What has happened to the Church universal, but especially in the USA, is the same as what we see recorded in the Book of Hebrews regarding the Jewish Christians. They had become "dull of hearing". The writer of Hebrews wanted to explain more fully the mysteries of the Kingdom but his readers had become sluggish in their reception. They had become lazy in their faith; therefore, they were considered babes needing milk, unable to digest the meat of the Word. They needed someone to teach them again the first principles. The writer chastises them, saying they are unskillful, unable to take in solid food. He says solid food is for those who are of 'full age', which they definitely were not.

The writer of Hebrews is pointing out to his readers the need for Spiritual Discernment. In other words, they need to hear the voice of the Holy Spirit and to humble themselves to be led of the Spirit. These are the Believers who are recognized as mature; who are disciples and who have become OverComers.

It is not those that hear only, that are mature, but those that do the Word of God. "Full age" refers to those that are mature due to habitual practice. Those of "full age" have made it a practice of obeying the message of righteousness and are able to discern good and evil. He encourages them to go on to perfection, meaning maturity.

The Apostle Paul prays for the Church at Ephesus, *"That the God of our Lord Jesus Christ, the Father of glory, may give to you the spirit of wisdom and revelation in the knowledge of Him, the eyes of your understanding being enlightened; that you may know..."* Paul was praying that the Church would not be "dull of hearing" but receive the Holy Spirit who is the spirit of wisdom and revelation and knowledge.

Paul is encouraging them to draw from the Holy Spirit in order that they might know what the hope of His calling is to them. Paul, like the writer of the book of Hebrews, knew his readers would be coming from different cultures. Therefore, they must develop their relationship with the Holy Spirit in order to know the will and the mind of God. What we are saying is; the disciple must have a supernatural experience with the Holy Spirit.

These new Christians were filled with a thousand questions. Some, like the Jews, had a faith in God but now needed to believe in Jesus Christ as their Messiah. Others had questions because they were completely ignorant of God; how to worship Him, how to live righteously and many other details regarding the Kingdom of God.

These first century Disciples of Christ were now facing persecution and trials that could never have been anticipated. **If they were to be disciples who would become OverComers, what they believed had to be more than a preference; it had to become a conviction.** They were facing the loss of friends and family, they were facing threats of imprisonment and even death. They needed a conviction within them that said, *"What I believe is the absolute truth".* Without that conviction, many would fall away and many did.

The Church today will soon be facing the same trials and persecution as the saints that have gone before us. They need to be more than followers of Jesus, they need to know and accept the principles that Jesus utilized in leading his followers through the process of Transformation, giving them the conviction to remain faithful to Jesus Christ. These same Kingdom Principles, when embraced, will cause you to remain faithful when hard trials come your way and when you are facing persecution.

Nevertheless, all of what is happening in the world today, the overthrowing of the world economies and the shaping of a one-world government, must occur as Satan is working his plan. The Scriptures themselves tell us in Rev 13:7-8 that, *"It was granted to him to make war with the saints and to overcome them. Moreover, authority was given him over every tribe, tongue, and nation. All who dwell on the earth will worship him, whose names have not been written in the Book of Life of the Lamb slain from the foundation of the world".*

It is sad to report that Satan has perverted the Church culture so that it now resembles the culture of the individual church, whether it is Catholic, Baptist, Methodist or Assemblies of God. Much of the culture that is within the Church now mirrors the culture of the world. If we do not recognize and accept this as a reality, we will never go on to seek Transformation.

Transformation –a new way of living

In the midst of all the coming chaos, God is raising up men, women and children who will be committed disciples, Believers who have a desire to be OverComers. If we look a little closer we must conclude that all of the marvelous things that OverComers accomplish are an overflowing of the person themselves.

It is the inner person that we must examine, his character, his spirit, his involvement with his God. WHAT HE DOES - IS -A RESULT OF WHO HE IS. Therefore, The Holy Spirit is transforming old wineskins into new wineskins- made ready for the New Wine.

The making of an OverComer is a little like a caterpillar turning into a butterfly. A caterpillar crawls upon the ground, over leaves and rocks. It can only see what is directly in front of it and only what is within fractions of an inch from its eyes.

What a contrast with the butterfly that has the freedom of the air. It can fly over the tops of trees and from flower to flower. Children and adults alike admire it for its beauty. It knows nothing of the confinement that is the life of the caterpillar.

When the caterpillar shuts itself away in its cocoon, it has no idea what will become of it or what it will be transformed into. We are not sure what exactly happens inside that cocoon, but this we do know; the caterpillar undergoes a *transformation* that will affect its life forever, never to become a caterpillar again.

We will also undergo a transformation when we become an OverComer for Jesus Christ. However, unlike the caterpillar, which goes through this change as a part of nature, we must make a deliberate decision. We must willingly lay down our "self" life in order to live the life of another. This transformation, like that of the caterpillar, will also affect our lives forever; we will never be the same person again.

What is it that determines our willingness to let the Holy Spirit transform us? Maybe Jesus had the answer when He said this about the woman caught in adultery, *"Wherefore I say unto you, her sins, which are many, are forgiven; for she loved much: but to whom little is forgiven, the same loves little"*. Here is the answer; it is in 'light' of our redemption that our love for God finds it roots and nourishment.

If we do not have a deep love for God, we will soon give up on the Transformation process and go back to being just a follower. We will be content just to make some changes in our lives.

God is not interested in changing us. He is interested in transforming us into His image. In this regard, we can liken our Transformation process to that of transforming an original 1932 Ford coupe into a V8 powered chopped and channeled Hot Rod. Once it is complete, you cannot undo and start over. This transformation is so much different from just adding a fancy paint job, mag wheels and leather interior. Those are just changes. Changes can be undone, but Transformation cannot.

The Transformation begins with our *involvement*. This is when we embrace the heart of the Father and align ourselves with His Grand Plan. Just as the caterpillar could no longer exist in order for the butterfly to come forth, so "self" can no longer exist in order for the "new Man in Christ Jesus" to come forth.

As we come to know Christ intimately "in us", His character will be revealed through our actions and our words. Others will look at us as if they are seeing Jesus. Jesus was a man of great faith; signs and wonders followed Him. As we strive to "know Him", our faith will also grow and the "works of God" will follow us!

Transformation is a creative act of the Holy Spirit. To become a son of God it will be because we are lead by the Spirit. In other words, to be lead of the Spirit is to mature. This is a process but it begins by having a kingdom mindset. By the grace of God, this is what I hope is imparted to you. By involving yourself in this transformation process, you will partake in the joy of participating in Kingdom Living.

Chapter Three

How Do You See Your World?

Obtaining a Kingdom mindset

Every event you experience in life shapes your *worldview* or *understanding of life*. It develops and takes shape and forms over time. As you grow spiritually, physically, mentally and socially, so does the formation of your worldview. We all perceive our world differently because of the differences of where we live, our education experiences, upbringing, and from what we hear from people we respect. Some of us cannot define or defend our worldview because we have never thought about it; we have just absorbed it from the influences that surround us. Nevertheless, we all have a worldview.

Our needs and wants (many of which come from our experiences) are what we deem most important and therefore drive the development of our own personal worldview. We use up large amounts of time, energy, and money traveling down many pathways that lead to nowhere because we really don't know what is of prime importance to us.

However, when Jesus draws us into His Kingdom-our worldview is turned up side down. The Holy Spirit comes to open our spiritual eyes. His presence redirects our needs and wants in such a way that we are willing to pay whatever price to walk in purity of life that is fitting for the sons and daughters of God.

Our worldview, whether religious or not, is a personal insight about reality and the meaning of life. It is often termed a "Life Understanding". It develops in part because we have sought some understanding of our own significance.

Whatever we do, we must come to that place where we agree within ourselves that what we believe to be the truth is correct or at least without consequences. If we do not, we are in disagreement with ourselves and when that happens, we can have no inner peace.

A worldview is a set of presuppositions (or assumptions) which we hold (consciously or subconsciously) about the basic makeup of our world.[i] A worldview is, first, an explanation and interpretation of the world and second, an application of this view to life.[ii] A worldview provides a model of the world, which guides its adherents in the world.[iii]

Whichever one you prefer of the three before mentioned definitions; it comes down to this: Our worldview is ever changing until we come to that place in life when we are at peace with ourselves in what we believe.

All worldviews or understandings of life are based on assumptions. Assumptions are beliefs without proof or something taken for granted. It is from these assumptions that we believe something is true or false, or somewhere in- between.

Jerry Simmons rightly points out, "the problem is; those assumptions, upon which we base our understanding of life, often go unchallenged. Therefore, we base our thoughts, feelings, and actions on false assumptions. Assumptions that are based on incomplete or faulty knowledge can and will most likely result in wrong conclusions."

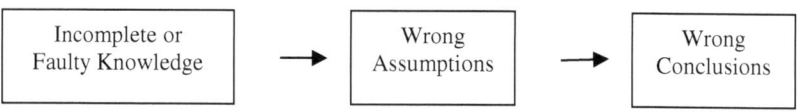

Culture: Prime source for our Worldview

The prime source for the development of our worldview comes from the culture of which we are a part. Cultures are described as the learned and shared patterns of information that a group uses to generate meaning among its members.

Within larger cultures such as that of a nation, city and region, there are also smaller cultures. In these smaller cultures, the members share beliefs in certain rules, gender roles, behaviors, religious beliefs and values. These cultural values combine to shape the individual's worldview and influence their interaction with others.

This is the point to comprehend, OVERCOMERS ARE THE PRODUCT OF THEIR CULTURE. You don't find apples on an orange tree. Neither do you find OverComers coming from a church that is more concerned with helping people to get a hold of the best life now or becoming a force for social change.

Culture is a breeding ground for the character of the people in that particular culture; therefore, choosing the correct culture in which to cultivate our worldview is of prime importance. Our culture is a major factor in determining what is important to us and then driving us to achieve.

Unknowingly we are forming our worldview, whether we recognize it or not, because we need a worldview to:

- Unify our thoughts about life
- Define the good life, that we might find hope and meaning in life
- Guide our dreams regarding our future
- Guide our actions

The Battle for the Mind

There is a conflict going on for our worldview. So what part does the MIND play in winning or losing the battle? The mind is the control center for all our dreams, hopes, fears and faith. It is here that we make decisions and vocalize what is in our heart. The mind is the center of our consciousness that generates thoughts, feelings, ideas, and stores knowledge and memories.

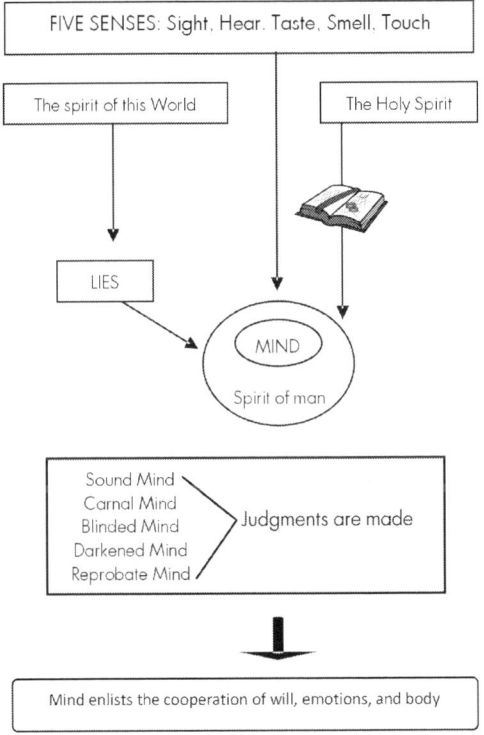

The Bible speaks of the Sound Mind, the Carnal Mind, the Blinded Mind, the Darkened Mind, and the Reprobate Mind. The Bible gives over 60 references to the word "think". Thinking is a process of the mind whereby we consider ideas and make judgments.

The mind is the collection point for the five senses as well as the spiritual influences, which enlists our will, emotions and body to perform acts that the mind has approved. Before we were converted and were "born again", the spirit of this world had full access to our mind. However, if we were brought up in the church, the Word of God could have affected our conscience and influenced our thoughts and behavior even before we were converted.

Satan's ultimate goal is to deceive us so that we willingly break the contract, the covenant that we have with God. This breaking of the covenant on our part results in the same loss of fellowship that Adam and Eve experienced in the Garden of Eden. Importantly, it is here that Satan wants to move us away from living a Kingdom culture to living a worldly culture.

The conflict is not between Jesus and Satan; that battle is already won. The real conflict rages here on earth between different worldviews that contend for our affection.

Satan knows that unless a Christian chooses and embraces a Kingdom Worldview and travels through the straight and narrow way, he is open prey that can be snared. Read what the Holy Spirit says about the Six Churches in the Book of Revelation as they deviated from the Plan that God had for them:

Ephesus	- The loveless Church
Smyrna	- The Persecuted Church
Pergamos	- The Compromising Church
Thyatira	- The Corrupt Church
Sardis	- The Dead Church
Laodicea	- The Luke-warm Church

As information is brought into the mind by our five senses and through our spirit, it finds a place to attach itself. If not, it is dismissed. We then make basic assumptions about the meaning of life, death, relationships and a million other things that ultimately affect our behavior. This behavior is reinforced day after day until challenged.

Why is it so hard for Christians and non-Christians to accept new ideas? Let us use a jar of jellybeans to try to understand our problem. Each of the jellybeans can represent a position (acceptance of a presupposition) that we have taken, that covers a million issues in life. They can range from our favorite color to being a Muslim or a

Christian. It can be from the kind of car we would like to drive to the type of person we want to marry. It could be a spiritual position, a philosophical position, it could be a social or an economic position we have taken.

These positions are accepted as truth. If not, then a conflict would arise within us and self-preservation does not allow this. The more firmly we accept our position as truth the more we are willing to defend it and even fight for it.

If the jellybeans (our positions on issues) are loosely packed inside the jar, another jellybean can easily take its place when challenged. Therefore, if we hold lightly to some truths, our positions or beliefs regarding those truths can constantly be changing throughout our lives.

If on the other hand, the jellybeans are packed tightly together, it then becomes much harder to displace one with another. This solidification of our presuppositions is sure to happen when we experience deep emotional, physical, social, and financial or even spiritual traumas. These traumas can come through nature (war, fire, hurricanes, and earthquakes), our personal environment (rape, robbery and assault), our education, or our family (divorce, separation or murder).

Again, if the truths we believe in strongly are a result of some traumatic experience, or come from someone we highly respect and trust or come from our prized education; these positions then have come about as from heat and are held together as if by super glue. This is like the jar of jellybeans that is left out in the sun and the heat has more or less cemented the jellybeans together.

Only one experience, however, can weld our worldview together so that it makes complete sense and bring us total peace. This experience is more valuable than any other is. That experience is the experience of Revelation by the Holy Spirit.

As a Disciple of Jesus Christ, can you define your new worldview? Are your jellybeans glued together so that no new thought has an opportunity to affect your life? Are you operating on incomplete or faulty knowledge?

How Do You See Your World?

[i] James Sire
[ii] Phillips and Brown
[iii] Walsh and Middleton

Chapter Four

You Become What You 'See'

Changing Our Worldview

Our motive and goal in this book is that we all may "see" God the Father, how all things are related to Him and to His purpose. In order to receive benefit from this study however, it may require a change in our worldview. How then does a change in our worldview come about? Adults are most open to new ideas when those new ideas speak about things that are most important to them. **We must understand; no change in our worldview can occur unless there is acknowledgement that our current view is wrong or at least based on insufficient information.** If our Worldview is to be radically changed, it must be by the Holy Spirit, through revelation.

Jesus appeared to Paul on the road to Damascus; Peter heard the rooster crow three times; Peter had a vision on a rooftop; King David had a finger pointed at him; Moses had two Hebrew men question his motive. In each of these cases, there had to be a rectification in their philosophy or Worldview. There was a pivotal moment that caused them to reflect upon and assess their presuppositions.

For too long we have been spoon-fed doctrine and told to, "just believe". We have been searching for a more meaningful life by attending conferences, changing churches, etc. without knowing that our searching must be for a deeper relationship with the Holy Spirit, who is the revealer of all truth.

The present world crisis is bringing people into the Church, some for the first time and many others are coming in from other religious backgrounds. As they come in, they bring in enormous amounts of wrong thinking that must be changed if they are going to put the puzzle of life together and have abundant life. There must be a modification in their worldview in order for them to be successful in their Christian walk.

A Challenged Worldview

Dr. C. E. Fast gave his life to Jesus Christ before he was 10 years old. He went on to college and then to Seminary where he earned his three Doctorate degrees and later in life he was awarded two honorary Doctorate degrees. He grew in prominence in his denomination and served the Lord in the largest Baptist church in Zion, IL. His reputation allowed him to serve in other high positions within his denomination as well.

The problem reared its ugly head when his wife, Edna, was introduced to a magazine published by The Full Gospel Businessman's Fellowship International. The small magazine presented articles about the Baptism in the Holy Spirit, speaking in other tongues and physical healings. Even though this was against what she had learned, something within the articles caused her to want to know more. She needed to learn more in order to satisfy the hunger that was now consuming her. She soon found herself speaking in other tongues and sharing her new experience with other women in her Baptist church.

Dr. Fast found himself in hot water when the church board found out what Mrs. Fast was doing. They quickly went to him and presented an ultimatum; have Mrs. Fast stop what she was doing (sharing her experience with other women) and renounce it as evil or they would force him to resign.

It is important to understand that Dr. Fast preached against this experience all his life. He did not have the experience himself nor did he desire it. He found himself in a very difficult situation. What was he to do? On the one hand, he could not deny the change he witnessed in his wife but on the other hand, everything within him said it was wrong. He would have to choose between the teachings he had received from his childhood through Seminary plus his own studies and his wife's newfound experience with the Holy Spirit.

If he chose to go along with the church board he would save his reputation, his standing within the denomination, and his pension (he was in his late fifties now). If he sided with his wife, he would lose his position in the church and all doors would be closed to him to pastor another church in the Baptist organization. To compound the issue, since he himself did not have nor did he desire this Pentecostal experience, the Charismatic and/or Pentecostals would have no need for him either.

He chose to go against the wishes of the church board. Even though he did not agree or accept for himself the experience as explained to him by his wife, he could not deny the new relationship she now had with the Holy Spirit. There was just too much academia, too much Baptist theology to overcome for him to accept it for himself.

Two long years went by of being a pastor without a church and being ostracized by former colleagues and friends. It was not until the Full Gospel Businessmen Fellowship International (FGBFI) had a retreat in Green Lakes, WI that Dr. Fast finally laid aside his Seminary training and opened his mind and heart. After three days of testimony and much prayer by others, he received that which he previously renounced.

He was finally able to exchange some jellybeans for others; jellybeans that had been cemented together by academics and years of preaching. For the rest of his life, God began to use Dr. Fast in supernatural and miraculous ways. His life affected hundreds of young men and women, including myself. Yes, these new jellybeans changed his life up until the day he died.

An Experimental Worldview

At the age of seventeen, Joni Eareckson Tada, became paralyzed because of an accident. She prayed for healing. However, she has remained confined to a wheelchair as a quadriplegic. When you read Joni's story you can do nothing but admire her. She has found meaning and purpose in her life despite all of the suffering, heartache and disappointments. We read in her story how God can work for our good and give us peace in the place which we come to accept.

She has developed a sensitive heart toward others who find themselves in similar conditions and has given them courage to go on and become productive, in spite of their circumstances. I can understand the position that she has come to regarding her paralysis. The following account is from an article that appeared in Moody Magazine, "Among Friends—Healing". It is a story of her struggle with faith.[i]

"The following event occurred after relating the story of her friend who was supernaturally healed. She asked, "Does this mean arise and walk miracles are for everyone?" Then she asks her audience, "Is God obliged to cure every sick person? I don't think so. The Bible doesn't teach it, and experience doesn't support it."

In terms of prayer, Joni states, "God gives two conditions if our prayers are to be guaranteed answers. We must be living in close fellowship with Him, and our requests must be in line with His will. Because God hasn't chosen to reveal every detail of His will to Christians, then we must leave our requests in His hands."

Joni says further, "It's more likely that he will glorify Himself through our suffering and this is quite a miracle. What if you are a Christian who is really trying to abide in Christ and you're still beyond a cure? If this is you, you're not alone. I can identify. But after looking everywhere else for reasons why my prayers were not answered, I returned to God's Word for a closer look. It was there I found something that shed light on not only the healing question, but also on the whole issue of why Christians suffer. If you have tried everything to be healed but nothing has changed, then has it ever really hit you that the reason you are in your present condition is that God, in His wisdom, wills it to be so?"

Joni has concluded, "Because God hasn't chosen to reveal every detail of his will to Christians, then we must leave our requests in his hands. He may remove suffering as a kind of sneak preview of coming attractions but it's more likely that He will glorify Himself through our suffering. And that is quite a miracle."

In the years following Joni's accident, her beliefs regarding healing and God's will solidified. They became as a jellybean jar sitting in the sun; the jellybeans melted together and nothing now or ever is going to change her position dealing with healing or in regards to human suffering in general. Joni had come to the place where she believed that she ("is beyond a cure") and that her condition is God's will. She can live with that (be at peace with herself). Here is the point to remember: We can go no farther than our Faith will take us. Joni has reached the limit of her Faith. We will and can act only on what we believe.

When we are predisposed to find our answers only within the realm of what is already accepted and unwilling to step outside our present worldview, we will accept anything whether it is true or not.

You will find our response to Joni's assertions on page 173

A Circumstantial Worldview

Stan is a Jewish man who grew up in New York City. In his home, he heard the stories that relived the horrors of the holocaust from his relatives. He is an Ivy League University MBA graduate whose family has come to believe God has abandoned the Jewish people. The stories of aunts and uncles that had witnessed the horror of Nazi Germany made a big impression on all of his family. He vividly remembers stories of how the Rabbis' fasted for weeks and prayed 24 hours a day, for days, only to become disillusioned when "their God had shut his ears to their cry".

At the telling of each story, another brick was added to the wall that was beginning to surround Stan's heart. It was not long before the wall was finished and he had sealed off any love for God that could penetrate his mind and heart. Stan still thinks of himself as a Jew. He observes all the Jewish holidays and even fasts on holy days. There is, however, no love for a God that did nothing for the Jewish people during those horrible days of the holocaust.

The stories from people Stan loves and trusts, plus the plain picture of history confirmed what he already had accepted as true. His jellybeans melted together and nothing is going to break them apart. The wall is built and no one can tear it down. He has closed his ears to everything except what he already has agreed to within himself.

Seeking your Worldview

The three foregoing stories model the case in point that it is difficult for us to change our worldview. We have already said that in order for us to find what our heart truly desires outside our present worldview, we must humble ourselves and be open to something new. It also demands a relationship with the Holy Spirit where by we are submissive to His leading.

Man is by nature curious. Nevertheless, because there is so much information out there, we cannot possibly digest it all. Because there is all this information and no central command post to filter out the truth from the false, many well intentioned Christians are being exposed to thoughts and ideas that sound true and good but are producing within them a watered down man-centered Biblical worldview. This incomplete worldview will lead to wrong conclusions and will keep them from maturing. While we must remain cautious, we must also be curious.

We have said earlier that what we consider most important in our lives will drive our search for a worldview What we really desire, even if we don't realize it, is dominion. Nevertheless, dominion is something that, either you have it or you do not. You are in control or you are not. We have to ask then; do men and women really know what is important for them to have?

We might have a limited form of control or dominion over our lives but it is only limited. Since man lost his dominion over the earth, he has been struggling and searching for the next best thing: freedom. However, to have freedom we must understand that freedom is a gift and is only given by the One who has ultimate control: the one in POWER.

How we think, act, and feel, comes from how we understand life—our worldview. It is the differences in our worldviews that lead us down different paths to what we believe is the place or the state of mind where we can find this freedom. It is while on our journey to find freedom that we spend all our energy and tax our ability and our heart.

We seek to be free from our daily grind, a job that we hate, the pain in our body, the pressures and stress of the job or family, the feelings of hopelessness, purposelessness, depression, and defeat, the worry of finances, children and sickness, the over-whelming guilt of adultery, pornography, lesbianism or homosexuality and the consequences of our lifestyle. Men and women want to be free from the bad relationships that they are locked into and from the control of others.

We want to be free to do what we want. We want to be able to choose the sacrifices that we will make. We want to be free to choose how we will spend our time and money and whom we will love or not love. We all want to be free, but man, without God, will always come to the wrong conclusions.

Mixing cultures does not work

The pathway that we take to find our freedom is more often, predetermined by our culture. When we come into the Church, we try to blend two cultures together, the World and the Kingdom of God. However, this does not work. There can be no compromise. One culture will always try to dominate the other.

The United States has been called the "Melting Pot" of the world. This designation came about because when people from all over the world came to the USA they did not establish cultural ghettos, they adapted to the language, norms and values that were already in place.

The reason so many people wanted and still want to come to the USA is base on the foundational principles that this country was built upon. The constitution says that each individual had rights given to him or her by their Creator that cannot be taken away. In the halls of government were found the 10 Commandments revealing its source of justice.

There were other identifiers for the outsider to see; its money is stamped with, "In God we trust". The pledge to the flag states that all citizens are a part of "one nation under God". The major universities were started to provide education to those studying for church ministry. Hospitals were started by churches to care for the sick. Schools used the Bible to promote reading and ethics. Even as late as 1958 schools gave early release to students, myself included, to attend religious education classes where they learned the major doctrines, creeds and tents of their faith.

Where is the clarity of American culture today? The above traditions are all but gone and so is our connection to the past. The United States was not so much a Christian nation but a nation that feared God. The Bible says the beginning of wisdom is the fear of God. It was not by accident therefore, that the USA became the greatest nation in recent times.

There are those in the world that want to keep the waters muddy and the eyes of our understanding blind when it comes to culture. There are those in our world that have fostered the idea of Multiculturalism, the belief that all cultures and beliefs are of equal value and have equal validity.

The truth is that all cultures, other than Kingdom culture, fail to provide a vision of a society, which incorporates faith, hope and love. They fail to offer a way of life for people from every race or economic and educational status to come and enjoy true abundant life. Kingdom culture is the only culture that so appeals to the heart of man that he will give all to obtain a right to be a part of it.

Please do not misunderstand me; the culture of the USA is not Kingdom culture. It does, however, allow the Church of Jesus Christ to openly reveal Kingdom culture to the world, hence the attack against America. The true attack, therefore, is really against God Himself.

Satan's attack on the culture of the Kingdom of God is deliberate and focused. He has one thing in mind; that is for him to retain and to even expand his kingdom and to finally include all earthly kingdoms under one rule, his. His kingdom is a kingdom of lawlessness while God's Kingdom is one of righteousness. Therefore, he is out to eliminate righteous living in the world.

Because of this, knowing Kingdom Culture is of the upmost importance. We must know how to respond when we find ourselves in situations like the above and to help others to find hope and freedom.

You Become What You 'See'

---

[i] Joni Eareckson Tada, "Among Friends—Healing" Moody Magazine

Chapter Five

Master Builders

Before Jesus left this Earth, He put everything in order so that His Father's Kingdom could grow in numbers as well as in maturity. Through His Church, the Father's kingdom would be made visible. Christ's Church was and is to be the instrument to extend the Father's kingdom and its success was His responsibility. His Father made Him His Lord and Christ and therefore, His final goal is to turn over all the kingdoms of this Earth, with all their authority and power, to His Father.

Jesus was under authority; therefore, He understood the importance of setting in place a structure of authority for His Church. We think of authority as hierarchical and therefore the one at the top is superior over the ones below. However, this is not the case regarding the relationship within the Godhead nor is it in the structure Jesus set up for building His Church. Nevertheless, the authority structure set in place by Christ has different levels that must be recognized if there is to be growth in the Church.

Jesus set in place 'gifts' to His Church. His gifts were not things, but men. Men who had been transformed by the very processes as outlined in this book. The Word of God that worked within them changed the thinking and the hearts of these men. His Spirit strengthened their spirits with might in their inner man. Peter gives insight into how this happened and gives encouragement to us today.

He writes in *2 Peter 1:2-4, "Grace and peace be multiplied to you in the knowledge of God and of Jesus our Lord, as His divine power has given to us all things that pertain to life and godliness, through the knowledge of Him who called us by glory and virtue, by which have been given to us exceedingly great and precious promises, **that through these you may be partakers of the divine nature**, having escaped the corruption that is in the world through lust".* Emphasis Authors

What an awesome statement; that we through knowledge, divine power, and exceedingly great and precious promises, may be partakers of God's divine nature. This is how these men and women, which were part of the five-fold ministry as given in Ephesians 4:11 were able to carry out their tasks.

The Ministry of the Word

This is a very important topic for us to consider before we discuss the five-fold Ministry. It is important because God's Word comes through man. We have the Bible –the Word of God- but unless someone preaches the Word, how will the unbeliever know the way of salvation and God's Grand Plan. Without the Ministry of the Word, there is no work. God, from the beginning of time "said" and the work was done.

In the Old Testament, God spoke through a person(s), the Prophet(s). The Word came to them and they spoke what was given. They did not add their own thoughts, feelings or opinions. If they had added their humanness to what they were given, it would have ceased to be God's Word.

A change came however, when Jesus appeared in the incarnation. Here is the difference; God again uses a person but the person of Jesus is the Word. The Word was righteous, holy, and full of wisdom. In the Old Testament God merely uses a man's voice and personality but in Jesus; human feeling, thought and opinion were expressed as one in the same. Moreover, they were the same, because His feelings, thoughts and opinions were the same as God's.

In Jesus, God's revelation of Himself to man became a man. Jesus is the express image of His Father and what He speaks and does is the same as what His Father would say and do. In Matt 5:21 Jesus said, "*You have heard that it was said to **those of old***", But Jesus now says, "*I say to you*". We must understand this profound difference. The first spoken word came from the prophets who spoke as they were instructed and spoke nothing more than they were given to speak. Jesus, however, speaks with authority, using His own feelings, thoughts and opinions. Through Jesus, the Father is getting closer to the fulfillment of His desire regarding the working of His Word.

The Father's intention is for man to be so radically transformed that Christ is completely formed in him. When he (man) speaks, he then would speak as an oracle of God. Those that minister the Word are to be so transformed. Here is the significant difference between Jesus and those God has ordained to minister the Word: When we consider Jesus, the Word of God made flesh; the Word came first and then was clothed with flesh. When we consider man, man came first and the flesh must be made to reveal the Word. His thoughts, feelings, opinions and actions must become the same as God's. What we will discuss in this book is the process of Transformation that brings about God's image being formed in man; man becoming as living letters to be read by all men.

The Apostle Paul understood the need for spiritual revelation of Christ. He wrote, *"The eyes of your understanding being enlightened that ye may know what is the hope of his calling, and what the riches of the glory of his inheritance in the saints and what is the exceeding greatness of his power to us-ward who believe, according to the working of his mighty power which he wrought in Christ when he raised him from the dead and set him at his own right hand in the heavenly places far above all principality and power, and might, and dominion, and every name that is named, not only in this world, but also in that which is to come: And hath put all things under his feet, and gave him to be the head over all things to the Church".* (Ephesians 1:18-21.

The five-fold Ministry

The principle that controls the Word is this; the Word is to be seen and touched by man. It must influence Man in all that he thinks and does. The men and women involved in the five-fold ministry are those that are so transformed by the Word; in other words, that which they speak is coming from God himself.

In this book, we will describe the transformation process by which we can judge those that claim to be Apostles, Prophets, Evangelist, Pastors and Teachers. It is the same process for all people. There are no short cuts. The only difference is the Lord has chosen some for different assignments then He has for others. With each assignment, there comes preparation and with every assignment comes the responsibility for its accomplishment.

The five-fold Ministry is just as important today as it was in the 1st Century. Unfortunately, as with the Laying on of Hands, casting out demons, and healing the sick; the five-fold ministry of Apostles, Prophets, Evangelist, Pastors and Teachers has been hidden until recently. Satan knows that the five-fold ministry is vital to the strengthening of every local church and Believer. Therefore, beginning with the 3rd century he tricked man into establishing the Apostolic Secession which teaches that the bishops replaced the Apostles. The Church set aside what Christ had set in place and it fell headfirst quickly until it finally entered the Dark Ages.

Much of the misunderstanding regarding the five-fold ministry is the direct result of Satan protecting his kingdom. The Church of the Lord Jesus Christ has the authority to pull down the strongholds of his kingdom therefore; he will do anything to prevent it from establishing the Kingdom of God in the hearts of men.

Jesus gave the Five-fold ministry to His Church in order that it might equip the Saints for the work of ministry and for their edifying until they all come to the unity of the faith in the knowledge of the Son of God. The Church is to bring each member unto a perfect man, to the measure of the stature of the fullness of Christ; that each member should no longer be children, tossed back and forth and carried about with every wind of doctrine. When this is accomplished, kingdom culture will replace the culture of this world.

Each member of the five-fold ministry has a grace that he is anointed to impart to the saints. This impartation, however, can only be achieved when the Saints are equipped to catch the 'Wind of the Holy Spirit'.

Jesus said, *"He who receives you receives Me, and he who receives Me receives Him who sent Me. He who receives a prophet in the name of a prophet shall receive a prophet's reward"*. An apostle cannot impart the grace within him if he is only received as a preacher. It is the same for any of the others in the five-fold ministry. If the people do not recognize the function of the one speaking to them, they cannot receive that which he is commissioned to impart.

A good way to describe the five-fold ministry is like what happens when you go to an optometrist to have your eyes checked for glasses. He first puts one lens into the machine so you can see the big picture and he then adds additional lens so you can progressively see clearer and clearer. So it is with the five-fold ministry.

The Apostle lays the first layer that reveals the big picture. The prophet comes along and lays down a layer that adds clarity regarding his function or task that the Lord has given him. The evangelist does the same and so on for the Pastor and Teacher. Just as you must have all the lenses in place to see clearly in the physical realm, we must have the complete five-fold ministry team involved in our lives in order to see clearly the full purpose and intent of the Lord in the spiritual realm.

The importance of the Five-Fold Ministry is similar to the need for two parents. Each parent brings to the child different and very important training.

Each leader must realize that, by himself, he is insufficient to bring about the maturity of the Saints. No leader can provide all the gifts and ministries that the people need that are under his care.

What we find in today's modern churches is that there are Pastors trying to do the task of two or three members of the five-fold ministry. They are the Evangelist, the Teacher, the Pastor and the Prophet all rolled into one. They are the lone single voice heard by the adherents or members. Some Pastors should be evangelist and others should be prophets but because the "Church at large" and even they themselves do not recognize these gifts, they are stuck where they are.

We must point out that even those involved in the five-fold ministry need the ministry of each other. They too are part of the body of Christ and each part of the body cannot exist by itself. The head cannot say it has no need of the toe.

Here's the point. When the Church only hears one voice, it is the voice of the grace given to that man. If a man is called by God to be an Evangelist then his calling (grace) will flavor every thing he preaches. If he is called to be a Pastor, then his calling will flavor every thing he preaches. If the Apostle does all the preaching, then his calling will flavor everything he preaches.

Here's the problem: the Church does not understand the differences between the gifts and therefore follows the man in the pulpit as if "this is all there is".

Some pastors feel that they need to protect "their" sheep or they feel they don't need anyone else to help them build their church. Jesus said, "I will build my Church" and I will give gifts of men to accomplish it because that is the only way to build my Church. Jesus will build His Church because His Church is built on the revelation of Himself.

To accomplish our purpose we must understand the purpose of Christ's coming; then we will be able to understand our calling. When we do, we understand what He meant when He said, "I will build my Church and the gates of hell shall not prevail against it." The gates of hell refer to spiritual opposition by demonic government. As Christians, you and I are involved in a spiritual war for dominion.

Without the five-fold ministry, the Church will not hear the whole story or see the complete picture. The Church will be fed but the diet will be insufficient and the body will be weak. The tree leans in the direction of the sun. If the Church only hears one voice, it will lean in that direction and the Church becomes departmentalized and will develop its own culture.

We make much commotion over the fact that each local church is sovereign or self-governing. With this sovereignty comes the freedom to accept Scripture as the local pastor and church board interpret it. They can organize how they conduct their worship service, their educational programs and whatever else they involve themselves. There are many examples of non-uniformity among churches that we all respect. Nevertheless, I respectfully submit that without the oversight of the five-fold ministry the Church has lost its faithfulness to the mandate given by Christ himself; that of preaching the Gospel of the Kingdom of God. **By rejecting the five-fold ministry, they have rejected Christ himself, who said that He would build His Church.**

It is not the intent of this author to bring a treatise on the subject of the five-fold ministry, but we must understand their importance and their function in order to appreciate the wisdom of our Lord. We will begin by explaining each function as it pertains to building up the body of Christ.

Each of the positions involve Leadership and Leadership is influence. You influence others for good or for bad. Although that sounds simple, it is more complicated than most people think. Everyone from the bully on the playground to the Apostle influence someone. The goal or purpose of that influence is what we want to consider next.

Some general comments regarding all those involved in the five-fold ministry - a true Apostle, Prophet, Evangelist, Pastor and Teacher knows that he should not think more highly of himself than he ought to think. He also knows that every good and perfect gift comes from God. He knows that he is no better than his Master and as his Master came to serve, he too must be a servant. Humility of spirit is the key word for these men and women.

It is important to point out that many are given visions and are in positions of leadership but not all are called to be an Apostle. Many may have the gift of prophecy but not all are called to be a Prophet. All Believers are called to evangelize but not all are called to be an Evangelist. Many are called to pastor or to shepherd others but not all are called to the responsibility of Pastor. Many are called to teach but not all are called to the responsibility of Teacher.

There is a heavy responsibility and accountability for all who accept the Lord's call to one of these positions of leadership. One should weigh the consequences of their possible failure seriously before accepting the honor. One can take upon himself the title but one cannot take upon himself the honor or the glory for the fulfillment of the task given.

There is a specific grace given to each member of the five-fold ministry. Each is responsible for imparting that grace to the Church. The Church has the responsibility to receive that impartation.

Apostle

The Apostle gets the most attention because we consider him the Leader. This is so because he can walk in all of the other four ministries. His responsibility and accountability are the greatest therefore; we should make sure we cover him in prayer. Honor is given to whom honor is due –and this is right- but he is just a man like the rest of us.

If any one sees the big picture, it is the Apostle and he is responsible for sharing that with the rest of those that are part of his team. It is to the Apostle that God reveals the deep mysteries of the Kingdom. Therefore, all others of the apostolic team need to be in close contact with the Apostle, for these revelations will govern and direct their lives. These revelations will then in turn direct their ministry to the Saints.

Acceptance of apostolic authority is voluntary. Those churches that are part of a denomination will possibly reject such a suggestion. Those that are hungry for a move of God and are burdened for the re-establishment of the Kingdom of God; they will embrace this revelation and seek out Apostles to whom they can attach themselves. It may be that their Bishop, superintendent, or sectional presbyter is the Apostle, or another, clothed as a Pastor.

The Apostolic Gift will make room for itself. The Spirit of God will cause others to recognize the Gift and the authority and Spiritual Gifts that accompany it.

The following is what others might see working in an Apostle:

A Visionary – sees things as God sees them and has the ability to cast that vision so that others buy into it

A Burden for the lost that is revealed by his love and sacrificial living for all people

A Burden for the building up of the body of Christ by teaching truths that transform and empower

A concern for the members of Christ body; each fulfilling their purpose

A concern for righteousness and holiness in the Church that is not afraid to discipline

An ability to know the heart of men and then to place them into positions of leadership.

Prophet

This might be the one gift given to the Church that is most abused. Because prophecy is thought of as insight into the future, many have prophesied falsely and because it sounds so godlike, it goes undiscovered as no one bothers to check it out. The Office of Prophet is more than foretelling, it is much deeper and broader than that.

The Prophet's function is a *ministry of restoration* through revelation. The Prophet must completely yield himself to the Holy Spirit, as his ministry is hard for the people to accept and therefore receives much opposition.

God, looking down from His vantage point and seeing that the Church is deviating from its course, brings about the ministry of the Prophet. Like a football coach whose team is playing terrible and losing games, he calls us back to basics, *makes a re-pronouncement* of God's purpose and thoughts. God is foremost interested in the fulfilling His purpose through His people and the Prophet keeps that before the people.

Like individuals, the Church can and does, become sidetracked and then begins to emphasis the parts instead of the whole. The Prophet recognizes that Purpose governs everything. His function is to present God's full, original and complete purpose according to the Mind of God. Like Moses, whose business it was to be exact in every detail of the tabernacle, the Prophet brings all the details before the Church in order that God's purpose will unfold exactly as His thoughts presented it.

The Prophet does not usually occupy a position in a Church. However, He many Pastors also function as a Prophet. He is a man of God who must come to God repeatedly to receive revelation. As he comes before God, the Holy Spirit speaks and spiritual things become fresh, alive and full of energy. The Prophet speaks only when he has something to say because it is the anointing that makes his words come alive, because they are coming from the living God.

This gift, given by Christ to the Church, is extremely important. To dismiss this gift as part of the ancient past or to blend it with the function of pastor or teacher is to deprive the Church of a voice that reveals truths hidden in Scripture that relate to the present day. Many Scriptures are not just for one period in history but are also for others. There were prophecies about Jesus, written thousands of years before He was born, that had meaning also for the day in which they were spoken. Just as in the days of the Old Testament, the Holy Spirit is unveiling the meaning of Scripture for us today through His Prophets.

As the Prophet brings light to Scriptures that have been in darkness until the present hour, Pastors and Teachers can now expound on these truths for the body of Christ. God can never be satisfied with anything less than the image of His son being formed in and then represented by His Church.

The following is what others might see working in a Prophet:

A burden for the truth of the Scripture – the prophet is concerned with bringing the spiritual implications of things before the citizens of the Kingdom. His burden is for them to have understanding of the significance of things in their spiritual value and meaning.

A burden for righteousness and holiness in the land with fearlessness in the fulfilling of his commission to speak for his king, even in the face of death

A Man of Prayer – Before he speaks, he spends time with God, allowing Him to see what God sees. It is only as he is in His presence does the revelation and the anointing come to him. He stands in the gap interceding and then as he hears from God he makes the pronouncement or judgment. His concern is for the people and as such, he is on the lookout for the approaching enemy and is ready to speak forth to those of influence to sound the alarm. A Prophet knows the mind of Christ, his king and is not afraid to let it be known.

Prophets benefit the Body of Christ by announcing, activating, imparting, confirming, and unlocking various times and seasons in Believers' lives (individually and corporately).

Evangelist

The Evangelist has fallen out of favor in recent years because of bad conduct by a few. The Pastor, who is the one who invites the Evangelist to come to their church, has never really understood their place in the five-fold ministry. Often the Evangelist is looked upon as one who unravels the cord that the Pastor has been weaving and then goes off, leaving the Pastor to pick up the threads. This is often true because the true Evangelist is in contact with the Apostle or Prophet and has received revelation that the Pastor does not have. Sadly, in years past, Evangelists were looking to build their own ministry.

The Evangelist is there to stir up the people (including the Pastor) to reach those who are under the domain of the evil one. He is there to awaken the Church to the power of the Gospel of the Kingdom, as seen when Jesus authenticates the ministry by signs and wonders that follow. For those that have not been Baptized in the Holy Spirit, he is there to stir up their spirit and prepare them for the task placed before them. The Gifts of the Spirit are in operation to make known the greatness of our God and to encourage the people to bring in their friends, family, coworkers and others to the meetings.

The Evangelist is part of the five-fold ministry team and therefore he is in contact with the Apostle and the Prophet. His ministry adds to the work that they are already doing in laying the foundation for kingdom ministry. Without his ministry, the people grow weak and lose their zeal for going out to deliver the captives and bring them into the kingdom. The people begin to rely on advertizing, the programs, the building and the great preaching of their pastor to bring the sinners into the kingdom.

The Church begins to lose its influence when the people lose the joy that comes to them when a sinner is saved. The Church becomes introverted and then is concerned with the blessings of the Lord instead of His Grand Plan for His people.

This is what we might see in working in the Evangelist:

A burden for those that are under the control of the Devil

A burden for the Church that has lost its desire to make the name of the Lord known

A desire to teach and train (tutor, instruct) the Saints to go out into the highways and byways to reach those not in the kingdom

He brings a message that captures the heart of God's people which motivates them to go out to invade, occupy and influence their culture and return the culture to the kingdom of God.

Pastor

The Pastor, in today's society, is the main man of influence in the Church. Everything rest and falls on what he does and says. His every word is taken as truth and that should weigh heavily on his heart.

We find the Pastor doing all those things that we normally consider them to do like: performing marriages, water baptisms, funerals, counseling those in trouble, preaching and the regular administrative duties that are required.

The REAL responsibility for the Pastor is teaching the culture of the Kingdom. Kingdom Culture is so different from the world's culture that without the Pastor's influence, families will be vulnerable to accept another culture, the culture of the World. Families are exposed to the world's culture at work, school, TV, sporting events, from friends, family members and even in some so-called Christian churches.

We look upon the Pastor as the Shepherd. He is to instill a faith into the sheep so that they know that all their needs will be met because the Good Shepherd loves them. Like a shepherd, he is to lead the sheep to quiet waters and green pastures. He is to feed them the Word of God that they might grow up into Christ. He is to take them to fields where they can lay down and find peace. He is to be on guard and be ready to protect them from their enemies. He is to make it possible for them not to be afraid, even in the mist of evil and turmoil.

He helps his people to have an encounter with their God that causes their faith to increase in order to make His Name known. He is to preach in such a way that the people develop a thirst and hunger for Righteousness. For, righteousness distinguishes the Kingdom of God.

This is a hard truth to swallow, but the majority of Pastors today are just being echoes of preachers from another generation. They read what others have said in commentaries and books about a certain Scripture and then repeat it as if it was their own. There is nothing wrong with repeating the words of others and being an echo, if we are receiving the same revelation that has come from our own study and from our relationship with the Holy Spirit. Pastors must seek a fresh word from the Lord.

This is what we might see working in the Pastor:

His biggest responsibility is to help his people work out their salvation so that Christ is formed in them. Sheep are prone to stray and wander; therefore, the Pastor must continually bring before them the consequences of sin.

He makes himself available for the people in his church.

The focal point of his ministry is the preaching on topics regarding everyday living such as: Mercy, Grace, Repentance, Holiness, Love, Marriage, Forgiveness, Humility, Relationships, Tithing, Physical Healing and Deliverance.

He makes the ministry of the Apostle, Prophet, Evangelist and Teacher available to his people.

He involves his people in missions, feeding the poor, providing for the homeless, helping those in drug programs, and ministering to those in prison. One does not learn to serve without serving or to give without giving.

The Pastor keeps the history of the people of God before them. Without a knowledge of their past, they will not know how they got where they are or if they are on track to where they are going.

Teacher

The Teacher works closely with the Pastor. He may have his own radio or TV ministry but he is accountable to the others in the five-fold ministry. Where he often goes astray is when he begins to align himself with a certain line of thought and it produces a following. He is then guilty of using his gift as a means of satisfying the flesh instead of bringing his audience to fulfill the purposes and intent of God.

The teacher has been given insight and wisdom to bring to the people. The meaning of scriptures, so that they clearly understand, is his to give. He makes Scripture applicable to their every day life so they can exhibit God's grace in their activities, whether family, work, social and even private.

Teachers must be careful of what they teach, as they are trusted as having insight that few have. *"My brethren, let not many of you become teachers, knowing that we shall receive a stricter judgment. For we all stumble in many things. If anyone does not stumble in word, he is a perfect man, able also to bridle the whole body. Indeed, we put bits in horses' mouths that they may obey us, and we turn their whole body. Look also at ships: although they are so large and are driven by fierce winds, they are turned by a very small rudder wherever the pilot desires. Even so the tongue is a little member and boasts great things". James 3:1-5*

The teacher must not only be a student of the Word but must wait upon the Holy Spirit in order to fit all the pieces of the puzzle together; seeing clearly the meaning of the subject matter. He has been given wisdom and understanding but he cannot rely upon solely his mind. He too lives in this world and is susceptible to the deceit of the Devil. He must be on guard at all times.

This is what we might see in working in the Teacher:

A burden for the people to walk in the truth of the Word

A dedication to study to make himself approved and helping others to do likewise

A student of the presentation, making things understandable to all; no matter their education, social or economic standing, mental capability or age.

Awaken a desire in others to be a student of the Word.

Master Builders

Chapter Six

The Weight of His Glory

His Burden is Light

Before we discuss the culture of the Kingdom of God, we must come to grips with the character of the citizens in the Kingdom. Kingdom citizens are the only people who will accept the culture of the kingdom and embrace it in daily living.

The road to the throne room is through a narrow gate that leads to the difficult way. The Beatitudes, given by Jesus, set apart the person who has fully understood the character of a citizen and the Grand Plan that the Father has for His children.

Beatitudes are more than nice sayings: they reveal the very nature of Christ Himself and therefore, the nature (character) of the Citizens of His Kingdom, the nature of His bride and the nature of those who will one-day rule and reign with Him. Unfortunately, the religious people have used the Beatitudes to deceive the people of the world and many in the church, to believe that God is concerned only with social issues and human character traits in these verses.

What is about to be revealed to you is the very nature of a king who reigns in righteousness. Therefore, to reign with Him, you must be prepared to give yourself totally to the work of the Holy Spirit who is the transformer of our minds and our hearts. If you have come to that defining moment and have gone through the gate to walk on the pathway that leads to the throne, keep in mind that there is a burden to carry.

Jesus said, *"All things have been delivered to me by My Father, and no one knows the Father except the Son. Nor does anyone know the Father except the Son, and the one to whom the Son wills to reveal Him.*

Come unto me, all you who labor and are heavy laden, and I will give you rest. Take My yoke upon you and learn from Me, for I am gentle and lowly of heart, and you will find rest for your souls. For My yoke is easy and My burden is light."

Jesus has the responsibility to turn over, to His Father, all the kingdoms of the earth at the end of this age. For that reason, He has established His Church to carry on His work until that time; she must be made ready to receive the new wine of the Holy Spirit so that the Glory of God will be revealed to the whole earth.

The glory of the Lord was first seen on Moses when he returned from being in the presence of God. Then we see the glory of the Lord revealed in the Temple that signified the presence of the Lord. Now it is time for the glory of the Lord to be revealed through the workings of the Holy Spirit through Christ's Church.

Now that we understand the absolute importance for each citizen to be transformed into the image of Christ, we can go on to examine the Beatitudes as a whole and each individually.

Jesus begins all the Beatitudes with these words, "Blessed are" and then He categorizes those who are blessed. There is a qualifier for each Blessing. In order to receive the Blessing, the citizens must have within themselves, a certain character quality. Since no citizen is born with these character qualities, an unwritten command is made that every citizen go through a transformation process.

To appreciate the Blessing one must first realize the source of the blessing. The Blessing comes from Almighty God alone, creator of heaven and earth and all that is above and beneath the earth. It is from His divine generosity and provision that Kingdom citizens are blessed. His Blessings are a gift that brings forth life to the receiver. Everything to sustain life, in spirit, soul and body has been given by the Creator. He has blessed his creation with 'life'.

These Blessings are a revelation of His Grace, His divine favor and his majestic power. They are a testimony of God's goodness and His great love for His people. The people who are blessed have separated themselves from the world. Therefore, the Blessing marks these as a special people to be a source of the radiation of His Glory.

As everything created was created for a purpose, each Blessing brings the citizen closer to the fulfillment of his purpose. God told them, *"Be fruitful and multiply; fill the earth and subdue it; have dominion over the fish of the sea, over the birds of the air, and over every living thing that moves on the earth."* (Gen. 1:28).

In fulfilling their individual purpose to extend the Kingdom of God throughout the whole earth, the glory of the Holy Spirit is manifested. It is through Christ's Church, by the work of the Holy Spirit, that the Glory of the Lord is going to be revealed in these last days.

Jesus speaks on behalf of His Father; therefore, His words are creative words as were the words of His Father. When Jesus pronounces a Blessing, He is giving to us a spiritual gift. He is speaking of what is not as if it were. To those that receive His words with faith, the Blessing is all ready theirs even though it may not be fully revealed.

There are four general characteristics regarding the Beatitudes that we must understand before we go any further. [i]

- ALL Christians are to have these characteristics revealed in their life, not just those who go on to sonship.

- ALL Christians are to manifest ALL of these characteristics. Each of the eight Beatitudes do not stand on their own. Each builds on the other and demands the other. The Beatitudes are a complete whole and you cannot divide them, even though some may be more recognizable than others may. The Beatitudes as a whole must become "internal" in us.

- None of the Beatitudes are what we might call a "natural" predisposition. These are spiritual qualities not natural traits. Nobody by natural birth is like a Christian. The Beatitudes are the result of the work of the Holy Spirit. They amplify the character of Christ within us.

- The Beatitudes are - the essential, utter differences between the Christian and the non-Christian.

Jesus, the King, spoke these Beatitudes that we might know the essence of the character of a citizen that aspires to become an OverComer to rule and reign with Him.

Christ lets you know that you are a citizen of the Kingdom and that you must develop your relationship with the Holy Spirit. He gives you a dream of having more than a good life as you live from day to day. He gives you a dream of reigning with Christ.

As we begin to exam each of these Beatitudes, let us image them as rocks, big rocks, not to big that we cannot carry them all in a bag, but heavy enough to know that they are a heavy burden. Let us imagine that we have this bag hung around our neck that is big enough and strong enough to carry the rocks as we put them in it one by one.

The 'burden' we are referring to is repeatedly told in the Old Testament. Moses is constantly telling the people of Israel to 'remember'. He lets them know that God is remembering His covenant with them. He tells them to remember they were once slaves but God brought them out by mighty miracles. He brought them out in order to bring them into a relationship. Remember, Remember, Remember. We must carry this burden, because we are so prone to forget. We are to remember that the life we are to live is the life of another, Christ in us the hope of Glory.

This is the reason for the rocks. The weight of the rocks will remind us that we are in covenant with the Lord of glory and that the glory of the Lord will be revealed through us as we are transformed into the image of the Lord Jesus Christ. We will act on His behalf and do mighty works in His name. This is the ministry of the Holy Spirit.

"If the law was glorious so even the people of Israel could not look upon Moses because of the glory of his countenance, which glory was passing away, how will the ministry of the Holy Spirit be not more glorious? For if what is passing away was glorious, what remains is more glorious... But we all, with unveiled face, are being transformed as in a mirror the glory of the Lord, are being transformed into same image from glory to glory, just as by the Spirit of the Lord." 2 Cor 3: 7—8, 11, 18

The eight Beatitudes are the necessary character qualities of one who is to reign with Christ. When we realize and act upon this truth, we will see the glory of the Lord. That is our dream and our focus.

Jesus knows to whom he is speaking. He knows that those hearing His voice are men and women in need of a savior and must be 'born again'. He knows, even though their spirit is renewed by their faith, the flesh will fight against their spirit. There will be continuing battles all their lives. Therefore, they must carry this burden of 'remembering' throughout their walk with the Lord.

He knows, that if they receive the Promise and catch the dream of the Father's Grand Plan, they must be fully transformed into the very image of Himself. They must become as He is.

THE EIGHT BEATITUDES

- Blessed are the **poor in Spirit** for theirs is the kingdom of heaven
- Blessed are those that **mourn** for they shall be comforted
- Blessed are the **meek** for they shall inherit the earth
- Blessed are those that **hunger and thirst** after righteousness for they shall be filled
- Blessed are the **merciful** for they shall obtain mercy
- Blessed are the **pure in heart** for they shall see God

- Blessed are the **peacemakers** for they shall be called the sons of God
- Blessed are those that are **persecuted for righteousness sake,** for theirs is the kingdom of heaven

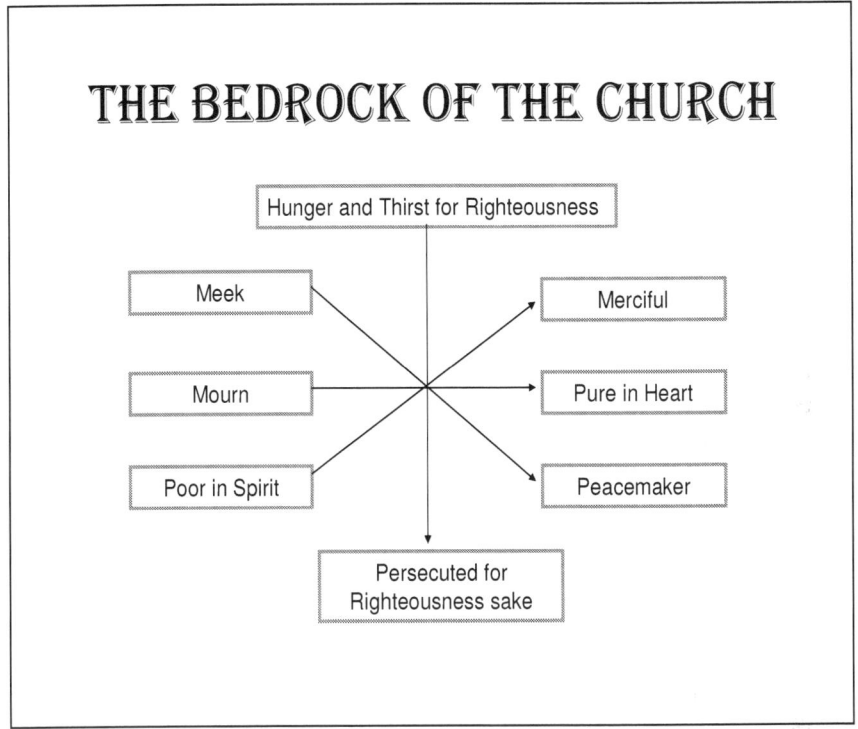

As you look at the diagram above, note that the Beatitudes on the left are connected to the ones on the right and the top is connected to the bottom.

The Beatitudes on the left involve our relationship with God. The Beatitudes on the right involve our relationship with others. The Beatitude on the top involves our own personal growth to fulfill our purpose while the Beatitude on the bottom involves the reaction of others as we venture forth to fulfill our purpose in the world.

"Blessed are the poor in Spirit for theirs is the kingdom of heaven"

The foundational criterion to rule and reign with Christ is our having received an abundance of grace and the gift of righteousness. It is not for the religious. The kingdom is not for the proud but for the humble, those that cry out for mercy.

Receiving mercy comes after we have seen our utter lack of righteousness within ourselves. We are all as naked before God with nothing in our hand that can erase our sin. There is nothing we can do to make ourselves clean. Our righteousness is as filthy rags. Our wickedness stands out like cow manure on a dinner table. There is nothing we have that can hide it or cover the smell. We must accept God's offer of a covenant of peace or suffer the consequences. We must accept His promise that He will put within us a "new" spirit.

The pathway to the throne begins with our first encounter with the Holy Spirit as He convicts us of Sin, Righteousness and Judgment. It is at this divine moment that the fear of a holy and just God enters our heart and we cry out for mercy. As we cry out, the Holy Spirit makes the love of God so very real to us in the person of Jesus Christ, the Savior of the World. With our forgiveness, comes a renewed spirit that enables us to have Spirit to spirit communication. This communication starts the flow of knowledge, understanding and wisdom in the revelation of Christ Jesus. It begins a love relationship with our God.

This encounter is the result of being 'poor in spirit' and is at the entrance into the kingdom of God. Jesus said, *"Most assuredly, I say to you, unless one is born again, he cannot see the kingdom of God."* This encounter is the start of a new life as a child of God. This encounter is the start of a relationship with our Father, the creator of all things and with His only begotten Son, the Word of God made flesh, the Lord Jesus Christ. This encounter is the first step on the pathway to the throne should we choose to travel the narrow way.

"Blessed are those that mourn, for they shall be comforted"

There is no rejoicing when you are mourning. Mourning passes after time when you lose a loved one, go through a divorce, lose a job, or go through some other traumatic experience. However, there is no real comfort that can be given by man; whether it is fame, fortune, or worldly pleasure when a man is convicted of his sin.

The only thing that will satisfy (comfort) his soul is the forgiveness of God, given to him when he repents (cries out for mercy). Jesus cried over Jerusalem, because they had rejected the Father's forgiveness that came through Him and Him alone.

Jesus did not come to condemn them but to restore them into the kingdom where they could find that which they so desperately sought. There is the mourning that settles our destiny. However, there is also the mourning that Jesus is concerned with here. It is as it affects our character. It is spiritual. It is an attitude NEVER found in the world. It is mourning over our sin in thought, word and deed. This mourning produces more than "I'm sorry". It produces a deep sorrow that causes us to seek for forgiveness and to change our ways.

The mourning that we are trying to describe is such that it sees not only the consequences of ungodliness but also the rewards of holiness. It sees a life, lived in the flesh, unable to please a holy God as well as a life full of Joy that results from a heart moved to mourn. Jesus demonstrates the mourning we are trying to describe as He prays, "*But now I come to You, and these things I speak in the world, that they may have My joy fulfilled in themselves. I do not pray that You should take them out of the world, but that You should keep them from the evil one.*

They are not of the world, just as I am not of the world. Sanctify them by Your truth. Your word is truth. As you sent Me into the world, I also have sent them into the world. And for their sakes I sanctify Myself, that they also may be sanctified by the truth. John 17:13-19

In every revival, the Church attracts the world ONLY as it functions as being unlike the world. This Beatitude then does have a great effect on matters of evangelism. We can reference the Welch Revival of 1901; bars shut down for lack of customers, police found nothing to do – there was no crime and families became families again. There are places in this world 'right now' that are experiencing such a reformation. It can happen in your city also.

Why do we not see more cities experiencing this reformation promised by the Holy Spirit? Why do so many people have no idea of what constitutes Sin? Why? The World has no idea of what Sin is because the church has watered it down so that no one recognizes it any more. That which is preached from the pulpits today is very different from what we heard from the prophets of old.

Tolerance and *Compromise* are the Buzzwords for the time in which we live and the Church has been following the World. It does not know what pleases the King of Kings or what grieves the Holy Spirit. It is looking for: "How to be a better me".

A mourning Christian, however, does not judge others but sees their lack of peace within, therefore he mourns for them. He sees the state of our society, our nation, and the World. He is disgusted, he is horrified (this is where the church stops) but he does not stop there; he mourns because of it. He understands what sin means to God – His hatred of it, His abhorrence of it. This is what causes him to mourn.

Lacking understanding of the true nature of Biblical joy has left the Christian community with not much to offer the sinner except a false hope. Real hope is full of joy that is unspeakable and full of glory. There is rejoicing even in the face of adversity. Real joy comes from a right standing with God and walking in all His ways.

You must mourn in order to be filled with joy and you must come under conviction before you can be converted. A real sense of sin must come before there can be true joy of salvation.

"Blessed are the meek for they shall inherit the earth"

What is truly amazing is that Jesus would humble himself to the extent that He (being the Word of God – therefore the same as God) would not use His power as God to further the work of God. Jesus emptied himself (laid aside His mighty power and glory) and became a man. What allowed Him to do the works of God? It was the working out of meekness. What we see in Jesus is meekness. This meekness in Jesus is the work of the Spirit. Jesus was meek because His dependence was always upon the Holy Spirit and not in His own human ability.[ii]

All through the Old Testament, we see men who had a heart for God but could do nothing until the Holy Spirit came upon them. It was then that they were able to do the Works of God. These ordinary men did miracles, however, these men allowed God to use them in a supernatural way.

Moses was looked upon as the meekest man on earth, but it took forty years on the backside of the desert for it to be finally seen. Sometimes that is what it takes to bring us to a total dependence on the Spirit's power.

Forty years earlier Moses had thought his position, his strength, his education and even his 'goodness' would get the job done but it did not work that way. It wasn't until Moses died to self that God was able to trust him with the supernatural and use him. It is as we put the "old man" to death, are we preparing our spirit to be in oneness with the Holy Spirit whereby God can do His work through us.

Being used of God to do the supernatural goes way beyond humility. Humility will cause us to see ourselves as mere men and no better than anyone else. Humility causes the grace of God to come to us and out of His grace; we find everything needed to live an abundant life.

54

Meekness, even though it involves humility, is not humility. Humility will bring us to our knees and we will cry out for help. There is no crying-out with meekness. With meekness, you have courage and boldness; there is no fear of the enemy because of our absolute dependence and trust in our God. We know the Holy Spirit is working through us to do the supernatural; it is not we ourselves.

Why is this Beatitude important to God and for us? It is because; it is *"the meek who shall inherit the earth"*. Isa 65:17 lets us know what our Father has prepared for us, *"For behold, I create new heavens and a new earth: and the former shall not be remembered, nor come into mind"*. There is a place prepared for us if we will allow the Holy Spirit to have His way.

The Holy Spirit is preparing a people who will do exploits for their king and in the end; they shall be co-heirs with Christ. The Holy Spirit will work through us to confirm the Word of God, which we speak, with Miracles, Signs and Wonders.

The world around us is full of people living in the kingdom of Darkness that know nothing of our God. We are commissioned to manifest the Kingdom of God to them that they might believe in Him. This we cannot do without having the spirit of meekest within us. It is only the Holy Spirit who can make real the love and power of our God.

Only the sons of God

Walking with the Spirit of God

Can manifest the Kingdom of God[iii]

Those who will inherit the earth – not heaven- are those that have proven themselves to be able to rule and reign. The meek are those that embrace the "internal Cross" and are led by the Holy Spirit. The meek will do exploits for their King because; it is not by power nor by might that we shall reign, but by the Spirit. Therefore, the Holy Spirit is working to effect a change in us; so meekness can come forth, allowing the Holy Spirit to lead and empower us.

The Meek man/woman is traveling the narrow and difficult way. He is dependent on Prayer. He dares does not trust or assert himself. He does not use his position. His strength is in his obedience and submission to the authority of his King. He is an Ambassador of his King; speaking and acting only on his behalf. The power that he commands is not his. The glory that will be revealed is not his to receive.

"Blessed are those that hunger and thirst after righteousness for they shall be filled"

When someone is completely satisfied, they have no more need, there is no room left for more, there is no lack. What a comparison to those that are starving, empty and in need of nourishment. The starving and parched can think of nothing else but to find food and drink. It is the same for those that are concerned about their soul and their relationship with their God.

The depth and breathe of our fellowship with the King is determined by the depth and breathe of the righteousness of Christ revealed in us. To those that hunger and thirsty for righteousness, Jesus says to them, "*I am the Bread of Life*" and "*If any man comes to me, I will give him living water*". It is only through our relationship with Christ are we filled, satisfied, complete and made whole.

David in Psalm 23 says of his God, "*He prepares a table for me in the presence of mine enemies; my cup runs over. Surely goodness and mercy shall follow me all the days of my life.*" This is the driving force for all those that desire to be an OverComer and rule and reign with Christ Jesus.

The foundation of the Kingdom of God is Righteousness and Justice. The scepter of His kingdom is Righteousness. Righteousness exalts a nation and when the righteous are in authority, the people rejoice. When the righteous rule, the city rejoices and is blessed by God because righteous people keep the truth.

With these truths in our heart, we are not only satisfied with good life but those around us are blessed. It is the responsibility of the Church to make these truths known to all men.

I have witnessed first hand, as I have been in countries around the world, the atrocities committed where wickedness abounds. Where does wickedness abound. It abounds in two arenas; first, where God is not present and the other, in places where a false religion dominates the heart and minds of the people.

We are seeing an increase of both these worldviews across the globe. Godlessness is fast growing in acceptance in America and false religions are fast growing in popularity in Western Europe. Islam is calculated to be the major influence in Western Europe by the year 2025.

Unless the Church unites under the scepter of Righteousness in the Kingdom of God, godless people will rule America. For both scenarios, Edmund Burke said it well, "The only thing necessary for the triumph of evil is for good men to do nothing".

"Blessed are the merciful for they shall obtain mercy"

You cannot give what you have not received. Those that show mercy are those who have received mercy. God has shown His mercy by holding back His anger and wrath because of our sin. He did not let his anger control him but let His love rule in His heart and in His actions.

Those that are merciful have experienced His forgiveness; the Holy Spirit has filled their heart with love so that they may show that same love to others. They respond now to others just as Jesus did because mercy is part of their spirit nature.

We can expect nothing of spiritual value coming from those that have not received mercy from God. All human beings are descendants from Adam and Eve, therefore their hearts are wicked and their righteousness is as fifthly rags, just as our hearts once were. They can expect only God's wrath when they are judged.

In order for the Sinner to know and understand the reality of God's mercy, they must see it at work in us. If we claim to know mercy, we must show mercy, not just to other Believers, but also to the ungodly. They must see the love of God working in us.

Because the flesh is still working in us, we still commit sins. Thank God, His mercies are new and fresh every morning that we might confess our sin and receive forgiveness. God is faithful and just to cleanse us of all our unrighteousness. When we show mercy, we shall always receive mercy.

"Blessed are the pure in heart for they shall see God"

Ps 24:3-6

Who may ascend into the hill of the Lord?

Or who may stand in His holy place?

He who has clean hands and a pure heart, Who has not lifted up his soul to an idol, nor sworn deceitfully.

He shall receive blessing from the Lord and righteousness from the God of his salvation.

This is Jacob, the generation of those who seek Him,

Who seek your face.

This is not a logically selected or preferred way of life amongst others nor is it the result of our circumstances, environment or education. It is a way of life that comes from the heart. We see in David, the Psalmist and king, a man who had such a heart.

Such a heart does not come without having first gone through the refiner's fire. When we consider metals and minerals; the purer they are (without contaminates), the more they are valued. These pure metals are the more costly because they have gone through a refining process. In the process, they tumble against each other to knock off the worthless material, and then they are washed and put through the fire until all the impurities are burnt away. Like jewels in a crown, it is only the purest that are fit for a King. It is no wonder that these people are called blessed.

Unlike metal that is placed in the fire with no escape, we can walk away at any time during the refining process. We will see in our discussion about the 'fellowship of His sufferings' many do not travel far down that road. Those that willingly go through the fire will find themselves face to face with the refiner, God Himself.

The 'pure in heart' hold onto the promise and the dream. Their faith and trust get stronger through every experience. They know that the refiner knows how hot the fire must be and how long to leave us in the fire. The one in the fire has gotten to know the comfort of God's presence and the sure hand of His love.

The 'pure in heart' have no greater desire than to be in His presence and see their God in all His majesty. They know that to manifest the Kingdom of God to the world and to extend the kingdom, it will take, not just knowing their God but also wrapping their arms around His heart. It requires that we live a pure and holy life.

but as He who called you is holy, you also be holy in all your conduct, because it is written, "Be holy, for I am holy." 1 Peter 1:15-16, NKJV

But you are to be perfect, even as your Father in heaven is perfect. Matt 5:48, NLT

"Blessed are the peacemakers for they shall be called the sons of God"

Our world is out of control with wars and rumors of wars. Some will accept peace at any cost. Reasonable people want a just and durable peace. Others want peace but only on their terms.

To live in peace means there has to be an end of hostilities. There is recognition of one being conquered and the other being victorious. There must be a surrender of one combatant before there is peace. Peace cannot be negotiated. One of those involved has to admit defeat or else war will be resurrected in the future.

It is interesting to note what Jesus said about Himself, *"Do not think that I came to bring peace on earth. I did not come to bring peace but a sword. For I have come to 'set a man against his father, a daughter against her mother, and a daughter-in-law against her mother-in-law; and a man's enemies will be those of his own household."* Matt 10:34-36.

Yet, in Isaiah 9:6, He is referred to as the Prince of Peace. In Matt 4:39, He commands the winds and says, *"Peace be still"*. In Luke 7:50, He says to the woman who washed His feet, *"Your faith has saved you, go in peace"*. Moreover, in John 14:27-28 He makes this profound statement, *"Peace I leave with you, My peace I give to you; not as the world gives do I give to you. Let not your heart be troubled, neither let it be afraid"*.

In the midst of our confusion regarding the two paragraphs above, He says to us, *"Blessed are the Peacemakers"*. In Matthew, Jesus is saying that, as King of a spiritual kingdom, He did not come to bring peace to this world system. In Isaiah and the verses following, He reveals that He has come to bring peace to the inner man, the spiritual man.

The inner peace, the spiritual peace given to Man will win over the world and an everlasting peace will replace evil. One thing is for certain, it cannot be disputed; whenever and wherever Jesus is present, there is either peace or division.

The reason people and nations are at war is because their ideologies differ or one has something the other wants and doesn't have. The beginnings of all wars begin in the heart and until the heart of one is changed, there will always be wars.

Jesus knows that the citizens of His kingdom are in a war, a spiritual war; a war that will last until the very end of the age. Therefore, Jesus makes it clear exactly who is our enemy and the strategies that he will use to defeat us. He also has provided the means to defeat our enemy.

This Beatitude speaks of two groups of people, Peacemakers and sons. Notice that Jesus puts them in the plural not singular. This is very significant.

To win a war and change a culture, it requires more than one person. To win requires an army of soldiers who are unified behind a leader and who will remain dedicated and loyal to the end.

Only the power of the Holy Spirit can bring an end to sin and release the captives. Only the Holy Spirit can bring an end to war, because He is the only one that can change a person's heart. That is why peacemakers are required to have within their character - 'meekness'.

Jesus said 'these' Peacemakers would be called the sons of God. There is no more awesome statement than this, to be able to say, "I am a son of God".

To be a Peacemaker is to be involved in an activity. You must be doing something. That 'something' is 'being about your Father's business'. In order to be called a son of God, a citizen has to undergo the transformation process that takes one through the first six Beatitudes. A son is mature, having grown through receiving knowledge, understanding and wisdom in the revelation of the Son of God. He has gone through trials and temptations and has been victorious.

Jesus' brought forth His Church with a demonstration of the Supernatural. On the Day of Pentecost, The Holy Spirit came down and the people witnessed flames of fire and the sound of a mighty rushing wind. His Church was born and a mighty army of kingdom citizens came forth. The Holy Spirit immediately began His work of transforming them into the very image of Christ, molding them into spiritual warriors, empowering them as a 'community' of Kingdom Believers to extend the kingdom of God.

They went forth, as sons of God, Ambassadors of the King and instruments of reconciliation in order that the world would be reconciled to God, their creator.

"Blessed are those who are persecuted for righteousness sake, for theirs is the kingdom of heaven"

As Jesus spent time with His disciples, He let them know what was to come as they followed Him. Note these verses:

- *And you will be hated by all for My name's sake. But he who endures to the end will be saved.*
- *Then they will deliver you up to tribulation and kill you, and you will be hated by all nations for My name's sake.*
- *And you will be hated by all for My name's sake.*
- *If the world hates you, you know that it hated Me before it hated you.*
- *But this happened that the word might be fulfilled which is written in their law, 'They hated Me without a cause.'*
- *I have given them Your word; and the world has hated them because they are not of the world, just as I am not of the world*

Hate is a strong word and most often results in war and death. This word is used from Genesis to Revelation; it reveals the evil that is in Men's heart.

In a cruel and wicked society, the righteous will stick out like a sore thumb when compared to those that are evil and love the darkness. When the righteous appear, light comes into a family, work place, playground or marketplace. The wicked do not want their deeds exposed because they are evil and they will fight against it.

Those that are righteous are not persecuted because they are sitting in their homes, in their churches, or hanging out with their Christian friends. They are persecuted because they are out in the world bringing light into the darkness, telling others of the goodness that the kingdom of God has come; challenging the sinners to examine themselves to see if there is any good in themselves that they might enter the Kingdom and be saved.

They know that, as evil people examine themselves, the Holy Spirit will find an opportunity to convict of sin, righteousness and judgment. It is because of this that they are persecuted. Jesus said, *"If they hated me, they will hate you"*.

"Jesus, when He had finished giving the Beatitudes, wasted no time in letting His followers know what to expect if they continued with Him. They could expect to be despised, mistreated and have all kinds of evil falsely said against them. They could expect to be counted with the prophets of old who were persecuted and killed; in that, they were to rejoice".[iv]

The Glory Life is Coming

We soon will be entering a time when what we have prophesied will happen. It will happen right before our eyes and we will be prepared for it or we will not.

The Holy Spirit has told us that, *"But know this, that in the last days perilous times will come: For men will be lovers of themselves, lovers of money, boasters, proud, blasphemers, disobedient to parents, unthankful, unholy, unloving, unforgiving, slanderers, without self-control, brutal, despisers of good, traitors, headstrong, haughty, lovers of pleasure rather than lovers of God, having a form of godliness but denying its power"*. 2 Tim 3:1-5

Perilous times are upon us. The Lord has called this ministry to, "Awaken the Church to the Joy and the Reality of Kingdom Living and the Adventure of being an OverComer". This, Kingdom Living, is nothing more than: Christ living (alive) within each of His citizens.

When God's people enter into Kingdom Living, the sons of God will manifest the Kingdom and the Glory of the Lord will shine for the whole world to see. I believe that what the Prophet Habakkuk said, *"For the earth will be filled with the knowledge of the glory of the Lord, as the waters cover the sea"* will soon be upon us and is at the very door.

The Spirit of God is moving upon the people of God in response to the prayers of the saints. The Lord is preparing laborers for the great harvest that is coming at the end of the age. He is raising up His five-fold ministers to lead His Church to victory.

Those that will be a part of the greatest move of God ever to come upon the earth will yield themselves to the Holy Spirit and hear what He is saying to the Church through His Prophets.

There is a peace, joy, and excitement within when you know where you are going and how to get there. You can focus on the journey and enjoy the ride, even if it is filled with bumps and difficulties along the way. The hardships of the journey do not get you down nor do they dampen your spirits because the reward is ever before you.

---

[i] D. Martin Lloyd-Jones, Studies in The *Sermon on the Mount,* 1959
[ii] Philippians 2:5-7 This is often referred to as "The 'kenosis' of Christ"
[iii] Apostle Jones Clark
[iv] Robert Farrier, *Greater Works then these shall You do,* Preface

Chapter Seven

Culturally Correct

Making the Kingdom Connection

H ave you ever worked on a 5,000-piece puzzle only to find it is next to impossible to put it together without a picture or at least have some clue to what it looks like? Even then, the picture must resemble something that we are familiar with or at least something, we can recognize. It is very much the same with life. We need a framework that ties everything together, something that allows us to understand our society, the world, and our place in it. It must help us to make the critical decisions, which will shape our own individual future. That framework is CULTURE.

George Barna in his 1993 book, *Turn-Around Churches*,[i] describes why he thinks some churches are growing and some are declining. In discussing the resistance to change he states, "Stalwarts in a dying church often argue that things will return to normal if the church can do a better job of doing what it has always done." On the other side of the coin, however, what he also found was that, "pastors of the new mega-churches attribute a significant part of their impact and growth to studying the ministry terrain and adapting their ministry practices to the needs and realities of the community context without undermining their theological beliefs."

The problem is that both views do not take into consideration the culture of the Kingdom that must be lived out. Both are trying to use religion as a means to meet the needs of people. They are both using a failed belief system as the foundation of their own brand of culture they are sprouting. By doing so, they are only adding to the division amongst God's people and still are not answering the deepest questions and longings of the human soul.

Christianity, as a religion and as it is experienced today in the Western world, is not the answer. Millions have left 'The Faith' to become agnostics, atheists, or adherents to non-Christian religions or cults. The Church has failed to make the Kingdom Connection. Christianity may be a religion but the Church is a community of the "called out" that are living for their King in a culture that He ordered and designed for His people.

Culture is a shared, learned, symbolic system of values, beliefs and attitudes. It is that which shapes and influences our perception and behavior—an abstract "mental blueprint" or "mental code." It is what shapes our worldview.

- Culture is something learned; it does not happen overnight. It is a process.
- The members of a society share culture. There is No "culture of one." This is important as it relates to the Church and our being involved in the Church.
- Culture has a pattern. People in a society live and think in ways that form definite patterns and are distinguished from other societies.
- Cultures are mutually constructed by all members of a society through a constant process of social interaction.
- Cultures come about through language and thought therefore they are figurative in nature.
- Cultures are arbitrary. They are not based on "natural laws" but are created, usually at the direction of those who are leading the society.
- Cultures are internalized; Worldviews (behaviors, attitudes, values) become Habitual. They are taken-for-granted and perceived as "natural."[ii]

In order to win the conflict for a worldview that enables us to have an abundant life and to be an effective minister, we must understand the Culture of the Kingdom of God. To do this we must know how it all connects to having a kingdom mind-set.

God has given to humanity, two institutions to make sure we have the structure that will enable us to have an understanding of the seven basic elements (covered in Chapter eight) that make up the culture of the Kingdom of God. The two institutions that shape our culture and therefore our worldview are: church and family.

The world is trying to use religion, or lack of, as a belief system to answer the questions regarding life, the purpose of life and the unknown of death. Like a puzzle, mankind's world has fallen apart and he has been trying to fit all the pieces back together again with the same results as Humpy Dumpy. The Church without Kingdom Culture is no different from that of any other religion.

Humpty Dumpty

Humpty Dumpty sat on a wall,
Humpty Dumpty had a great fall.
All the King's horses, And all the King's men
Couldn't put Humpty together again!

Catching the Wind

The responsibility of fashioning Kingdom Culture has been given to the Holy Spirit. Just as He was given the responsibility of bringing the creative Word from heaven to form the heavens and the earth, so He is shaping and molding the culture of the Kingdom into the life of the Church.

He does not work alone, however, so in order for the Church to complete its assignment, Jesus gave Apostles, Prophets, Evangelist, Pastor and Teachers. This five-fold ministry team is charged with the task of making sure the culture of the Kingdom of God is extended throughout the whole earth. The reason, for the five-fold ministry, is so that the responsibility does not rest on anyone person. Each member of the team has a part to perform in the bringing the body of Christ to maturity.

The best way I know how to relate the work of the five-fold ministry is by a personal experience. When I was ministering in the Finger Lakes region of New York State, my son, Steve and I bought a small sailboat. One day, he and I went out to Seneca Lake at Geneva, N.Y. Seneca Lake is a spring fed; cold and deep lake nestled between two hills. Because of this, strong gusts of wind would suddenly sweep down over the water and catch many unsuspecting, untrained, unqualified and unwary sailors unprepared for the danger that could lie ahead. Of course, I'm speaking of myself.

The sail is the heart of a sailboat. Without the sail, a boat is dead in the water. What is most important to a sailor is the ability to catch the wind. The wind causes the boat to move and fulfill its purpose. It is the skill of the sailor, however, that determines the direction and speed of the boat, because he determines the sail's ability to catch the wind. Even when there is only a little wind or even when there is not a favorable wind, a good sailor can go forward by adjusting the sail.

The purpose of the five-fold ministry, in its simplest terms, is this: They are to help the members of the body of Christ to 'Catch the Wind'. In this simple act, they demonstrate to the Church their own submission to the 'the Wind' and are an example to the saints.

The majority of Churches have opted to teach everything under the sun EXCEPT how to 'catch the wind' (the moving of the Holy Spirit) and kingdom culture. Is it any wonder that we are where we are with no power and no vision for the future except heaven? If we are truthful with ourselves, we must admit that we can hardly recognize any difference when the Church is compared with the world.

Having a Form of Godliness

Satan already knew that he was in trouble when he stirred up the people to crucify the Messiah, the King of God's people. He went to work immediately and released the spirit of religion and we see that it has taken over the Church in all countries of the world.

The Apostle Paul recognized this 'take over of the Church' even in the 1st century and sent a warning to the Church. In 2 Timothy 2:26-3:5, he writes, *"and that they may come to their senses and escape the snare of the devil, having been taken captive by him to do his will.*

But know this, that in the last days perilous times will come: For men will be lovers of themselves, lovers of money, boasters, proud, blasphemers, disobedient to parents, unthankful, unholy, unloving, unforgiving, slanderers, without self-control, brutal, despisers of good, traitors, headstrong, haughty, lovers of pleasure rather than lovers of God, having a form of godliness but denying its power. And from such people turn away!"

What does this mean, *"Having a form of Godliness"*? This is the spirit of religion. It means that the Holy Spirit is not in control of their life. He is not there to Transform and Empower. When He does come, there is denial, grieving, a quenching and ignoring of the power of the Holy Spirit. Religion robs God's people of ministry. People now come to the Church to receive and get their needs met instead of to be encouraged to GO and minister to others.

Religion steals the power from the Church. Because religion has within it no power to resist sin, there is within the church the same sin as in the world: adultery, lies, stealing, perversion, gossip, coveters, idolaters, drunkards, revilers, and extortioners. Because of the Holy Spirit is not moving in the lives of these people, their Praise is empty and unacceptable to the Lord. Paul makes a strong statement in Galatians 5: 19-21 1 Corinthians 6: 9-10 and in when he says, *"those who practice such things will not inherit the kingdom of God".*

In Genesis 1:1 it says that the Earth was without form – void. Then the Holy Spirit moved in and began to give it shape and to make it come alive. There was darkness until the Holy Spirit brought light. There were no stars, no air, no clouds, no grass or trees, no animals, no people until the Holy Spirit took the Word of God and gave it form.

The Holy Spirit did nothing until Almighty God spoke and the Word came forth. The Bible says He was hovering over the face of the waters just waiting for Almighty God to speak the Word so he could go to work.

God's form has design and purpose. It is the same for everything that God has created. It is the same for the Church that Jesus said He would build. We are the Church. He is giving His Church form.

He has given His Five-fold ministers the gift of the Holy Spirit that they might bring to the Church the form that Almighty God has had in His thoughts before the foundation of the World. Therefore, He is charged with *transforming* us into the very image of the Son of God and creating Kingdom Culture in the Church.

Paul was given this insight and shares it now with us in Romans 8:19-30. In verses 19-20, he gives God's end purpose that the Holy Spirit is charged with; transforming us (Kingdom Believers – OverComers) into sons of God. The whole of creation is waiting expectantly for us to be revealed and to for us to deliver it from the bondage of corruption into the glorious liberty of the sons of God.

The end of the Holy Spirit's work will result in Christ's Church being conformed to the image of God's Son, that He might be the firstborn among many brethren. He has called us and justified us that we may also be glorified.

Let us make sure then that we are living in the reality of the one who lives within us and living the culture of the Kingdom of God.

---

[i] George Barna, *Turn-Around Churches,* Introduction page 12
[ii] The definition of culture came from a variety of sources with no one source making a major contribution

Chapter Eight

Seven Elements of Culture

Kingdom Culture

A kingdom has no stronger influence upon another than through its culture. Its values, morals, citizen's behavior, dress codes, music, religious practices and more express who they are and even more so, who they represent. Jesus made known the power, the quality of life, and the blessings of being connected to His kingdom. Kingdom Culture offers to all the citizens a way to experience it.

Seven basic elements make up a culture, any culture and these are what we want to focus on. They are: Government, Economic System, Social Organization, Customs and Tradition, Language, Art and Literature, and Religion.

Government and Economic System, however, are not normally included in the definition given by Sociologists. I did conclude, while traveling overseas and paying particular attention to the culture of the country in which I was ministering, that these two elements influence and therefore determine the shape of culture more than anything else.

What I also concluded was that; it is the primary responsibility of the Church of the Lord Jesus Christ to explain and demonstrate the culture of the Kingdom of God. Everything else church leaders do is of lesser significance. The Church has preached on these topics from time to time but they have failed to make the Kingdom connection.

1. Government

The king makes his will and desires known through a government that he creates. Whoever rules over a government, exercising its authority, is the one that has the most powerful influence on the kingdom's culture. The government exercises its influence by controlling and administering public policy that will affect all members of the society.

The government of the kingdom of God is built upon righteousness and justice. Righteousness is the golden thread that is woven into every fabric of the kingdom. It is the factor that influences all the motives, thoughts, feelings, and actions of the king and the citizens of the kingdom.

In the Kingdom of God, our governmental ruler is Jesus Christ. He is our King. He rules over His kingdom that is subject to His laws. He shows no partiality. Each citizen is subject to the same set of laws and He judges each citizen with the same holy justice. He sits on the throne of His Father and rules now, not the earth, but the affairs of kingdom citizens. He rules the hearts of those that have entered into the Kingdom by being "born again." He will in the end, however, rule over the whole earth and judge ALL men everywhere, both those who are alive and those who are dead.

The dominion of the earth has been given to the citizens of the Kingdom who are to use His authority to extend His kingdom. All authority is His and His alone; we are to use it to carry out His Father's will here on earth.

To function within the Kingdom of God, we must understand how God's government operates. The following Chapter (nine) will give a description of the nine fundamental activities of government.

2. Economic System

There are many different economic systems in the world, Capitalism, Socialism, Communism, and even a mixture of types. The end purpose is to control the lives of people. Those in power control the financial centers of their society.

To various degrees, the individual is unimportant as a person and is useful only as an insignificant part of a jumbled mass of insignificant parts. Individuals are seen as workers, part of a mass, who are tolerated as a needed ingredient to accomplish the common good.

The 'mission' for every economic system is to control or regulate the production and distribution of goods and services. The 'purpose', however, is to control the final output or the medium of exchange. In the world's view this is know as currency. In the Kingdom of God, we know it as Faith.

Faith is the basis of how all of Kingdom Culture operates, including economics. FAITH is at the heart of our relationship with the triune God. Without FAITH, nothing happens in the Kingdom of God. God operates by FAITH. Even in Creation, the Word was spoken and by faith, the worlds were created. We, as citizens live by Faith.

We must see FAITH as it is used as the medium of exchange in the Kingdom. In the physical realm, we recognized money or gold as having a standard of value and therefore we use it as a medium of exchange. In the spiritual realm, FAITH is not just about believing, but about exchange; it has valve.

Every culture has a medium of exchange, whether it is gold, silver, potatoes or paper money. It is what that culture recognizes as having great value and can be used as a means of exchange throughout that nation, country or kingdom. No nation can exist without a medium of exchange.

When I was in Poland, before the Iron Curtain came down, I could not buy anything with American dollars except at what they called "Dollar stores". It was illegal for the citizens to have "Dollars". I could only use their "Zylote" to purchase items that I wanted. In every country where I have gone it is the same; I could use only the currency that is acceptable and recognized.

The principle is the same in the Kingdom of God where the medium of exchange is FAITH. Faith is of the greatest value and even Peter said that is why our Faith is tested; to see its REAL value. Is it fool's gold, 8 caret, 10, 14, 18 or 21-carat gold?

Just as the quality of our FAITH is important, so is the quantity of our FAITH. How much faith do you have, no faith, a little faith, much faith? Jesus, the Son of God and our King said, "According to your faith be it unto you!" Jesus could do nothing but heal a FEW sick folk in Nazareth because there was no faith.

In this world, we are so used to using money as the medium of exchange that we don't know how to use Faith or how to operate it. We have reduced FAITH down to something we can understand; putting it in earthly or worldly terms. We understand it as a belief, a confidence, and a mental acceptance of something.

In the physical realm, if you need a new roof for your house, you need the amount of money demanded by the contractor. If you do not have it (money), the citizen of the Kingdom of God can go into the spiritual realm. Here he petitions God for the faith needed to receive the needed money.

God does not just send this money from heaven just because you asked. He requires the quality and quantity of faith that will allow Him to release into the physical realm (into your hand) the amount of money you need to pay the roofing contractor. Your faith says to you, "God has heard me and He will provide".

How He does this is up to Him. He may make it possible for you to get a raise, your brother may offer to help with the cost, the contractor may lower the price, or a friend, to whom you loaned money 20 years ago, may suddenly repay you. Who knows what God may do?

If you need a healing for cancer, you need the faith that is required. Just because you were healed of a headache yesterday does not mean that the faith that you had yesterday will enable you receive a healing for a cancer today. You must present the faith needed before God in order to receive what you need.

How do you get faith? You get faith the same way you get money to pay a doctor bill; you work for it. There is only one source for FAITH; it comes from the same king that provides what you need, King Jesus. It is something like buying from the "company store". The company pays you for the work you have done and you buy what you need from the company.

The author and finisher of our FAITH is Jesus Christ. He is the Word made flesh. FAITH comes from the Word and as you spend more time mediating on the Word, allowing it to flood into your very soul (this is the *work* part), your heart begins to focus on the love and power of your King. Your hand now reaches out to receive what you've asked for because you know your faith is sufficient to cover the cost. Revelation springs up in your heart and you know that you know that God is pleased with your FAITH (quality and quantity).

There is another aspect involved in the economic system that goes along with FAITH. Jesus said, *"Give and it shall be given back"*. Sacrificial giving is the heart of the Father; giving of oneself for another just as He demonstrated in the giving of His only begotten Son.

Much more is said on this important topic in my second book, *"Greater Works Then These Shall You Do"*. There is a worksheet at the end of the book.

3. Social Organization

People who are a part of or submit to Kingdom Culture need to connect with others of like attitude and mind-set. We individually are saved by grace but together—we subject our wills to the will of our King; and say to our Father in heaven, *"not my will but yours be done"*. It is together that we fulfill the purpose for which we are created.

Culture comprises many things but the bottom-line is that it is all about relationships. Therefore, when outsiders to the culture of the Kingdom are given the opportunity to look into the Kingdom, what they see is something that is a complete opposite to the culture of this world.

The first relationship we see in Scripture is that of the family. God created Adam and gave to him a wife. God told them, *"Be fruitful and multiply; fill the earth and subdue it; have dominion over the fish of the sea, over the birds of the air, and over every living thing that moves on the earth."* (Gen. 1:28).

God established the family unit to express Kingdom Culture. The family is to be FRUITFUL (fulfill its purpose), MULTIPLY (have innumerable descendants), FILL THE EARTH (be productive, bring into the storehouse, an abundance), SUBDUE (use your authority), and HAVE DOMINION (prevail against, reign, rule over, maintain order).

Within this extended family culture, we see the love that Kingdom people have toward their king. We also see the love that the people have toward one another. They love even their enemies and do good toward them that hate them. What the outside world witnesses is Christ revealed in the saints of God as they are transformed into the image of their King.

Here we see the Fruit of the Spirit being manifested in the relationships between family, friends, business associates, school children and other community members. If there is one element of the Kingdom that is missing in the Church today, it is the teaching and practice of living where the Fruit of the Spirit is witnessed.

The Fruit of the Spirit is produced only in relation to other people. It cannot be produced or practiced between God and us alone. When the Fruit of love, joy, peace, patience, gentleness, goodness, faithfulness, humility and self-control are apparent to all, we know that the Holy Spirit is in the life of a person and He is at work in them.

4. Customs and Traditions

Customs usually come about because of events, location or personal likes or dislikes. Some customs are ordered by those in authority to give remembrance to great men or to God, while others just happen. The customs and traditions found in Kingdom Culture are not a result of just a one-time event but are a result of habitual practice becoming the usual way of acting or responding in a given situation.

When our children see those in the Church living-out the culture of the Kingdom, they accept this behavior as NORMAL. When those in the world see this behavior, they recognize the cause and effect relationship—obedience brings blessing.

We hand down to the next generation our traditions and customs regarding holidays and celebrations so that they have a connection to a lifestyle that we cherish. We hand down statements of belief and wisdom that will benefit and bring blessing to our children and pray that they will past these down to their children.

We cherish our *Traditions* because they link us to our past. *Customs* are important to us because they reveal and reinforce the principles and values by which we live. This is why the enemies of Christ wish to tear them down. I.e. School Prayer

5. Language

Language is more than just a means of communication. People that speak the same language bind themselves together in thought, word and deed. Language greatly influences our culture by and through our thought processes because language predetermines what we see in the world around us.

Words are symbols of ideas and have definitions. They shape our way of thinking. When we use one word to describe something and someone else uses another word to describe the same thing, we are not looking at the same picture that is formed in the mind.

Words, when translated into another language can have an entirely different meaning and convey something quite the opposite from that which was intended. Words must be understood because they reveal what is in the heart of the person speaking. This is why I have to depend on God to choose my interpreters for me when I am overseas.

Language also acts like a polarizing lens on a camera in filtering reality. A polarizing lens eliminates the glare that reduces depth perception, distorts your view and colors. Therefore, language allows us to see the real world because we can only understand our world through what we can express through our words.

YOU + YOUR LANGUAGE = YOUR REALITY

The Old Testament was written in Hebrew, which is a pictorial language. When a word is spoken, it almost immediately appears as a picture in your mind. While in the New Testament, which is written in Greek, a more precise meaning appears that differentiates it from another, it is more black and white. When we combine our study of these two Testaments, a clearer picture is presented of life in the Kingdom of God.

The language of the Kingdom and the meaning of its words do not come from the earth but from heaven. Our communication comes from shared experiences, shared facts, ideas, and events that have been interpreted by the Holy Spirit. Worldly eyes have not seen nor did their ears hear what the spirit has revealed to us, the citizens of the Kingdom. Jesus spoke in parables so that those in the world would hear but not understand, would see but not comprehend.

74

The Kingdom is for its citizens, not for the world. The Kingdom is for those that have entered into it by being "born again." The language of the Kingdom of God is what moves us and transforms us into the image of Christ. When we speak the Word, we enter the spiritual realm and with this in mind, we can have whatever we say. (See Mk 11:22-24).

6. Religion

Every culture has a religion that is accepted by the majority of people in the society (a more or less ordered community). It gives people something to cling to when life brings events beyond their understanding. It consists of universal patterns of beliefs, values and behavior.

These patterns of a culture's religion are systematic because their manifestations are regular in occurrence and in expression and the majority of the members of that religion share them. Within all religions, however, not everyone complies with all the doctrines prescribed. There are differences of interpretation of the principles and meanings put forth. What is of great importance is that when the people have a close tie toward their leaders and with each other, their core beliefs are held more strongly.

All religions present to their adherents, symbols and rituals that make life meaningful. The Catholics kneel and make the sign of the cross when they come into the church sanctuary. Baptists stand when they read the Bible in church.

Cultures endorse a system of religious symbols, along with religious actions to establish powerful, pervasive, and long lasting moods and motivations. In other words, these symbols help to construct how a society will view the world around them. It helps in providing a worldview that includes—a god. In the Kingdom of God, we share not a religion but a relationship with the king.

7. Art and Literature

Art and literature are ways and means that we humans use to express what is in our heart and mind. We all are not artists, architects, musicians or storytellers but we can and do live vicariously (experience through someone else by using the power of our imagination) just as if it has happened to us.

We buy the music, books, and go to movies that reflect what appeals to us and say what we think and believe. We imagine ourselves in situations and places, that only art and music can take us. Culture is what produces the art and the music and therefore controls the dreams and aspirations of the people.

Our God is the creator of all things, even our ability to be creative. There is not anything made that He did not create first in the spiritual realm. Everything that is created in His Kingdom is noble, just, pure, lovely, of good report, virtuous and praiseworthy. These things lift our souls and spirits high and bring us joy, peace and the abundant life.

The Bible is our standard for literature. The Bible opens our heart and our mind to things way beyond the capabilities of our humanness. Within its pages, the emotions of the heart come to life, all the wonders of science ignite our imagination and we see the power of the universe enacted right before our eyes as people are healed, demons are cast out and the dead are raised.

Community

In order to tie the purpose of culture together, we need to look at the concept of community. Culture is what makes community work. One would think that if everyone has the same culture there would be total unity. This would be true; however, not everyone accepts in totality-the whole culture.

In recent years, the kingdom of darkness has introduced the concept of multiculturalism into the world politics of western civilization. This concept fosters the idea that many cultures can get along together without conflict. It says that every culture has values that will add greater value to the whole. Because of its acceptance, many long-standing societies that were once thriving and peaceable are now coming apart at the seams.

It is interesting to note that Multiculturalism has been rejected by eastern cultures. Their strong religious leaders have understood the perils of opening up the doors to people of other belief systems and have therefore kept their cultures intact.

Contrastingly, the nations in Europe have rejected the message of Christ and the teachings of the Bible; they have embraced multiculturalism to the extreme. By doing so, they have allowed the tenets of The Earth Charter to gain a foothold and are now finding themselves on a fast spiral downward as a culture. The United States is fast approaching the point of tearing apart its Christian belief system and will soon lose its place on the world stage because of the acceptance of this deceptive and evil concept.

When America was a young nation and when people from the

countries in Europe and other parts of the world came, they recognized a common language, work ethic, religion, government, and economic structure. Many of the customs and traditions were combined and accepted and therefore became as one. The people, who came here, became AMERICANS. They left the culture of their birthplace behind. They had a dream of a better life in a new place. They came here and began to organize as a community of Americans. This is now being replaced by the concept of Multiculturalism.

The goal for both the Church and family is community. God's Grand Plan is for us to rule and reign with His Son over this earth. He instructs us to have the mind of Christ: that means having the Wisdom of God. Kingdom Culture reveals the wisdom of God. Wisdom, when applied, will solve all our human problems, explains the love of God, reveals the rewards of obedience, gives understanding of the laws of the universe, shows how to maintain relationships, and makes clear how to conduct ourselves in the presence of God.

Kingdom Culture is the vehicle that brings about community and community is the vehicle that communicates the wisdom of God to the world.

It is only when we have a Kingdom mind-set will we be able to work toward community. In the 1st century, knowledge of citizenship in the Kingdom was fundamental therefore, anyone who was "born again" was a part of the church community. When people were added to the Lord, they were added to the Church. When they belonged to Christ, they belonged equally to His body.

This early Church was bound, one to another by a covenant, a covenant of Love. Their love was translated into commitment. This commitment was their obligation to service and self-sacrifice. Community was possible because they were able to overlook one another's faults and shortcomings. Their commitment was directed to the spiritual growth of one another.

The Community that they enjoyed together, allowed spiritual growth to take place. When there is mutual respect for others, an atmosphere abounds where the Spirit of God can bring about the forming of Christ in His body. The Kingdom Culture of the Church is what the world still needs to witness. The world, however, can never realize its desire for community because it will not accept Kingdom culture.

We cannot superimpose Kingdom Culture on top of world culture and call it Christian. There is an absolute difference between the two.

We cannot bring the world into the Church nor can we take the Church into the world. The two are separate. The cultures are diametrically opposed to each other.

From Paul's first letter to the Corinthians, we note that the severest punishment for a believer who committed a gross sin was to be excluded from the Church. These early Christians looked to the Church for strength as they belonged to one another. To be left out of the community meant coming out from underneath the umbrella of fellowship.

The early Church had all things in common. Today this is most often thought of only in regards to the distribution of wealth. The distribution of wealth was a direct result of their culture. Nevertheless, the context that brought about this act of generosity is much broader than this because there was a greater dynamic going on then the surrendering of one's possessions.

The people assembled there had ALL things in common. This meant that their faith was common. Their love for one another was common. Their values and strength of character was common. Their worship and service to their God and King was common. Their culture was common. What they had was common-unity-COMMUNITY.

Chapter Nine

Kingdom Government

Fundamentals of Government

In Chapter eight, we discussed the seven major elements of Kingdom Culture. That which is of primary importance, however, is Government. It is from the seat of power or the throne that the other six find their shape and form.

As we look closer, we find there are nine fundamental branches that make up the tree of Government. The tasks performed by those involved are vital to the orderly operation of a nation.

I. Constitution and Laws

A major concern for any government is its relationship with its citizens. This relationship is spelled out in some form of Constitution along with its Laws. This is even more paramount in the Kingdom of God because, as we said from the beginning, it is all about Relationship.

God knew that man's rebellion against His rule would put him under the rule of Satan. His heart would be changed from a heart that had affection toward God to a heart of stone. Instead of having a heart of "giving", he would now possess a heart of "getting". Without God his new depraved heart would cause him to put himself first (self-centeredness) before all others and the passions of his perverted soul would dominate him throughout his life.

When God was ready to reveal to the whole world His Grand Plan, He chose a people who would embrace His promise by entering into a covenant with Him. Therefore, He miraculously brought them out of bondage from the Egyptians and in bringing them out, He formed them into a nation of people and He himself became their King. They were not a kingdom at that time because; at the beginning they had no territory. God, however, did give to them a promise of land that would be theirs forever.

To show His great love for them and to reveal to them that He was indeed their King, God entered into a covenant with them. Their part of the covenant was to keep the laws that were given to them through Moses. These laws, when obeyed, would allow peace and harmony to exist and would bring forth a blessing and not a curse to those within the Kingdom that God was establishing in the Promised Land.

The covenant, with its terms and conditions, became their constitution (the document outlining the laws and principles by which they were to be governed). God put His wisdom of government into a book (we now call it The Bible) that was to be read and explained to each generation so that each citizen could know their God (king) and understand their responsibility as citizens.

The laws that Moses brought down from the mountain and the subsequent laws that were written down in the Torah, pertained to every area of life. The laws, when obeyed, revealed the love, compassion, wisdom, and the power of their God Jehovah. Their obedience to the Laws brought blessings to the people and showed the kingdoms of the world the greatness (power and wisdom) of Israel's God.

Laws were instituted for their good; not to limit their freedom but enable them to enjoy life and have it more abundantly. When God's laws were broken; suffering, sickness and pain were the result. This was not a result of God's anger because of their breaking the covenant, but just the normal consequences of their behavior. It was when they rebelled and set up other gods to worship that the finger of God came down to punish them.

There were also dietary and sanitation laws that protected the people from disease. When they were not followed, sickness and even death resulted. Obedience resulted in health and safety for all.

II. Taxation

There are certain components of a kingdom that are best done by the King and his government. These areas are functions that are not for one person or family but are for the good and benefit of all those in the kingdom. These include roads, a water system, defense, commerce, and other areas that develop as a society enters the technological age.

In order for the citizens to take some responsibility for their own welfare, the King taxes the people and spends the proceeds accordingly. A good king does not need to ask the citizenry for permission to do what he thinks is best for the kingdom. A parallel thought is this; parents do not ask their children, the parents just do what they think or know what is best for the whole family.

Our covenant with an invisible God is first spiritual and then becomes physical, so taxation (or tithe) is first spiritual and then becomes physical.

Jesus did not come to abolish the Law; He came to fulfill it. The tithe is incorporated into the Law, therefore, Jesus saw this as part of

His governmental structure and as a part of the government of His Church.

However, tithing is much more than just giving money to the Church, that's earthy. Tithing is the signifying of our approval of the way our King is benefiting us through the services He is providing. We are showing our gratitude and thanksgiving though our obedience. It is showing our allegiance and loyalty to the King. It is a requirement for all citizens. It is not optional; it is demanded.

When we gladly bring our tithes to the Church, which is His governing influence here on earth, God makes His provisions available to us and rebukes the devourer for us.

When we do this collectively and when it becomes a part of our culture, the other nations will call us blessed because they will see the goodness of our God.

It is important to note that the tithe is 10%: that is for everyone; it is not progressive. The payment of the tithe is for the poor as well as the rich. There are no free rides, no free lunches. Everyone pays. It is their responsibility. Obedience brings the blessing.

The Churches that do not teach tithing as an element of being a responsible citizen of the kingdom, do their people a great disservice and bring upon them great harm and pain. The judgment that will come upon them will be severe because Christ's Church is to be a light and salt in the earth that they might reveal the real King to the other nations.

III. Security/Protection – Expansion

A king builds an army to protect that, which is His. He defends His territory against all invaders, whether physical, psychological or spiritual. He is just as protective over the work ethic, talents and abilities of his citizens. These resources reveal His wealth and enable His citizens to carry on commerce and trade with other nations. A king does not willingly give these up without a fight.

When a good king has a powerful army, his citizens are secure in knowing that when they are under His rule, there is safety. A king not only provides for national defense but also makes provision for individual citizens to defend themselves against personal attack that would destroy their desire to be a part of Kingdom Culture.

Our King Jesus knows that we *"wrestle not against flesh and blood but against principalities, against the powers, against world rulers of this present darkness, and against hosts of wickedness in heavenly places"*. He, therefore, has given us the needed armor to, not only protect ourselves but to go on the offensive. He promises that He will never leave us nor forsake us. He promises victory in the fight.

Some kings just want to hold on to what they have. Others want to take what belongs to others in order to increase their wealth and power. Our King however, has a mission to take back what was stolen from His Father when Adam, God's representative, gave away the keys to the kingdom through deceit and a false promise of freedom from the control of God.

Therefore, Jesus is gathering the "called out ones" to be a citizen's army. After Jesus described the character of the citizens of the kingdom to His disciples, He tells them that they are to be salt and light. They are to keep safe the culture they enjoy and to extend their culture to others as well.

The army of God is not to just to hang on to the gains it has made but is to extend the king's kingdom through the pulling down of strongholds and attacking the enemy wherever he rears his ugly head. Just as light is not to be hid, His kingdom, its culture, is not to be hid inside the four walls of a local church. We are to take the battle to the streets and let the His light shine.

IV. Justice

Life without justice is a life of torment for those that are righteous. The wrong doer must be punished and righteousness upheld. Justice makes the terms—right and wrong—meaningful. Justice knows no skin color, gender or religion. Justice is not negotiable.

Even though it may seem as if the ungodly are not punished, our King Jesus lets us know that all will be judged, the ungodly for their rebellion and the godly for their works of righteousness. At the end of life, there is justice for all. In the spiritual and the physical realms alike; what we sow, we shall also reap.

Kingdom Culture must reveal this aspect of life. It is what the world desperately needs and longs for. They see the injustice of those that have their own personal agendas. They see the immorality of those that we once admired. They see the poor, elderly, the less intelligent taken advantage of, and no one to take up their cause for justice.

Kingdom justice teaches us that each one of us is RESPONSIBLE for our own deeds. We are held ACCOUNTABLE to others for our behavior. Justice is for ALL-no one is above being judged. The Bible is our standard for justice.

Our Kingdom Culture demands that we must take a stand against injustice. If each local, individual sovereign church is promoting its own culture by staying silent, then Kingdom Culture has no voice. Today, so many pastors are remaining silent when the cry for justice would give the Holy Spirit an opportunity to speak to the ungodly and bring conviction of sin, righteousness and judgment.

V. Commerce

I have been in the poorest of the poor countries on earth. From my advantage point, I could see that the reason for their poverty is based on the political, economic, social, religious, communication and technological structures that are in place. All of the above either hinder or advance the ability to conduct Commerce. In other words, their culture determines the blessedness or the curse that comes upon them.

In the Kingdom of God, Adam and Eve were told, *"Be fruitful and multiply; fill the earth and subdue it; have dominion over the fish of the sea, over the birds of the air, and over every living thing that moves on the earth."* (Gen. 1:28).

The English term, 'fill the earth' loses much of the forceful meaning of the Hebrew word, **male'** used in the above verse. It is a term that represents the omnipresence of God, *"Do I not fill the heaven and earth? Says the Lord."* Jeremiah 23:24. He 'fills' the whole earth with His glory and is visible by the glory cloud that 'fills' the tabernacle.

When God told Adam and Eve to 'Fill the earth', He was telling them to be productive. They were not just to sit around and do nothing; there was work to be done. They were to be productive, produce by labor, an abundance (actually an over abundance).

In the Kingdom of God, each citizen is given by God a means to produce. Each person has an ability or talent making it possible for him/her to be productive and earn an income. However, whatever their ability or talent, they are to be compensated accordingly. Their gift from God will make a way for them. Each can find contentment with their gift.

The execution of Commerce in the Kingdom is based on principles that God has given to His people. Some of them are:

- *"Honor the Lord with your wealth, with the firstfruits of all your crops."* Pro 3:9

- *"Lazy hands make a man poor, but diligent hands bring wealth".* Pro 10:4

- *"Wealth gained by dishonesty will be diminished, but he who gathers by labor will increase".* Pro 13:11

- *"Of what use is money in the hands of a fool, since he has no desire to get wisdom".* Pro 17:16

Commerce deals with the exchange of goods and services, from the producer to the final consumer. The basis for this exchange is this; what is produced has value. It encompasses the trading of something of economic value such as goods, services, or information, between two or more entities.

This exchange, in the kingdom of God, is based on each person's integrity. Integrity is the bedrock of commerce in God's Kingdom and must be a part of the culture that we reveal to the world, by both the Church and the Family.

The world revolves around commerce. Each individual finds fulfillment in the exchange of what he has to offer (his talents and abilities) for something that he finds important. Commerce in the kingdom is a part of experiencing the Abundant Life.

Closely related to commerce is the economic system of a culture. As citizens of the Kingdom of heaven, we are involved in the two different economic systems. The world's culture operates on a medium of exchange or currency: money. Kingdom Culture operates on a medium of exchange, which is FAITH. Jesus operated in both and showed his apostles how to do it. Let us follow their example.

VI. Education

Much of the present day dilemma in our American society is the result of the Church allowing culture to be taught at the discretion of the arm of government known as the public schools system. The public schools are guiding the morals, attitudes, knowledge, and decision-making of eighty-nine percent of our children instead of the Church.

As a result, when our children go to the Universities, the godless culture learned in grade school is reinforced and even expanded upon. These graduates then go on to be the business leaders, schoolteachers, mothers, and fathers of our grand children. Is it any wonder that the ball of godlessness keeps on rolling?

Satan has deceived the church once again in order that he can keep his kingdom safe from being over-taken by the Kingdom of God. Satan will do whatever it takes to keep the light from shining into the darkness of his kingdom and to make sure our salt has lost its saltiness.

The National Education Association in 1951 proclaimed, "It is important that people who are to live and work together shall have a common mind, a like heritage of purpose, religious ideals, love of country, duty, and wisdom to guide and inspire them."[i]

The message of their civics handbook was fortified with selections from Old and New Testament passages, the Ten Commandments, the Lord's Prayer, the Golden Rule, the Boy Scout Oath, and patriotic songs. Because it looked good on the outside, the Church bought into it and handed the formulation of our children's worldview over to the godless. We were deceived.

Gone are the Sunday School classes of the 40's and 50's. Gone are the Sunday night and Wednesday night services to teach the saints the Word of God regarding - the necessity for and the opportunity for corporate prayer. Gone are the Levites of Ezra's day that made sure every man, woman and child understood the Word after the reading of the Law. (See Nehemiah 8:7-8).

Education is the responsibility of the family and is reinforced by the Church. Education is more than reading, writing and arithmetic; it is the means of formation of the whole person. Because parents have lost their own way in this godless world, our children have no moral compass to look to in order that they maintain their true north heading.

VII   Covenants

To insure the continuation of the present government for future generations, those taking office take an oath of allegiance saying that they will uphold (support and defend) the constitution and laws of the Land. These oaths are important because the one taking the oath possess authority and power to direct and lead.

The oath is similar to a covenant but without the penalties associated with breaking a contract. However, an oath speaks volumes of the integrity of the one guaranteeing his word. God has made many oaths and with all, He was and is found faithful; even when the Nation of Israel deserved to be destroyed God kept His oath. An oath cannot be altered or changed; it is permanent.

In others words, the one who made the oath must keep it regardless of circumstances. James gives us fair warning regarding making an oath when he writes in James 5:12, *"But above all, my brethren, do not swear, either by heaven or by earth or with any other oath. But let your "Yes" be "Yes," and your "No," "No," lest you fall into judgment."*

A covenant is different in that it is the joining of two or more people into a binding relationship. It could be a pact between equals: brothers, friends, marriage, or between neighbors. It also could be a pact between unequals: stronger/weaker, superior/inferior. It could be between nations but it also could be between individuals. It is usually the weaker who initiates the agreement by coming to the stronger or it could be the stronger imposing his agreement upon the weaker; in either case, the stronger dictates the terms and conditions of the agreement.

In regards to our covenant with God, it is a covenant between UNEQUALS. What is so unique about our covenant is that the Stronger has come to make a covenant with the weaker. It is His desire to have a relationship with the lesser: the Holy with the unholy. We did not choose to come to Him to appease His Anger or to seek His blessing. He comes to us and offers Himself to be our *protector*, our *provider*, and our *friend*. He comes to us and offers forgiveness in order that He might have a relationship. He comes to us and reveals His desire to be our Father, not just our Creator.

God has a purpose for His creation. He created man to have dominion over His Kingdom therefore, He offers man a covenant, allowing him to return and fulfill his purpose.

God has sealed this covenant, first with an oath and then with the blood of His only begotten Son. God is faithful to keep His part of the agreement. The question remains: will we keep ours? *"The secret of the Lord is with those that fear Him, and He will show them His covenants."* (Ps.25:14).

The agreement between God and man is not one-side therefore, we must understand the terms and conditions, as well as the blessings and the penalties.

1. Covenants consist of terms, conditions, and promises of the agreement.

2 There is an oath signifying both individuals will keep the terms of the agreement.

3. There is a curse (penalty) for each one, should they break the agreement.

4. There is a sealing of the covenant by some external act such as the blood sacrifice (signature).

In Exodus 19:3-6 God gives Moses a promise: *"Now therefore, if you will indeed obey My voice and keep My covenant, then you shall be a special treasure to Me above all people; for all the earth is Mine. And you shall be to Me a kingdom of priests and a holy nation."*

Notice that the Promise is tied with a condition. This is the condition: if the children of Israel obey God's voice and keep His

86

covenant, God will keep His Promise. God has much at stake here. He is looking way beyond the Nation of Israel. He expects Israel to separate itself from other nations because of their special relationship with Him. They were to be a holy people because He is Holy. Because of their separation from the other nations, their culture will be entirely different. The other nations would see that they are blessed and they would learn of the true and living God. They would come to hate them for it.

In Exodus 20, God begins to put down the conditions that they must follow and gives Moses the Ten Commandments to give to the people. In Exodus 24:3; 7, the people made a solemn oath of obedience to follow the Lord.

In addition to keeping the Ten Commandments they were required to offer animal sacrifices. These sacrifices were a reminder that justice must be served in order for God to forgive their sin. The sacrifices were gifts given to show honor to God. The sacrifices were an indication of their desire for intimancy, their confession of sin and desire for pardon. The sacrifices were offered in a spirit of faith, following the example of Abraham when he offered Issac. The sacrifices offered were the lambs without blemish, the first fruits and others. The point to be made is that they were costly to those making the offering.

The Nation of Israel did not escape the penalties for breaking the covenant. The Curses found in Deuteronomy 28 were harsh and terrible. It was not until the Nation of Israel repented and called upon God that they found deliverance and rest.

God's covenant with us is our guarantee that every promise He has given to us will be fulfilled. It is the Title deed to our inheritance. If we are thinking from a Man-Centered Worldview, we might be thinking of earthly blessings such as heaven, prosperity, health, deliverance from evil situations. If we are thinking from a Kingdom Worldview, we are thinking of strength to live a holy life, escape from temptation, being filled His righteousness, abounding in peace, love and joy, growing in the grace of God, and maturing into Sonship, a position of dominion.

When we instruct people to ACCEPT Jesus as our Savor, what does that mean? What does that mean to those that come forward to the alters in our churches or at our dining room table?

Do they understand that they are entering into a relationship that must be developed and are not just being a part of a different religion? Do they realize that God will not allow them to mix their former religion with their relationship with Him?

Do they understand that they are entering into a covenant relationship that has penalties if not adhered to? Do they understand they must "die to self" in order for them to fulfill their part of the agreement?

Do they realize that their relationship requires that they fear their God, walk in all His ways, love Him, serve Him and keep His commandments?

The covenant that God offers us is a blood covenant. God's son shed His blood, but He calls us to offer our bodies as a living sacrifice. God has made all the arrangements for the execution of the covenant. All we need to do is trust in Him and love Him.

VIII Citizenship

From the beginning of this book, we have learned, 'It is all about relationship'. It still is about relationship but we now need to consider what our relationship with the King additionally means to us. What we are now talking about, of course, is our life as a citizen of the Kingdom. It is not a matter of living according to laws, creeds, or identifying with some doctrine of faith.

Too often the message of the Kingdom has been turned from a life-giving source into a religion that has no power. Even the name, "Christian" has become a religious term whose adherents have no concept of the Kingdom of God, the joys of citizenship or the privileges of living under a new government.

"Now therefore you are no more strangers and foreigners, but fellow citizens with the saints, and members of the household of God; having been built on the foundation of the apostles and prophets, Jesus Christ Himself being the chief cornerstone; In whom the whole building, being fitted together, grows into a holy temple in the Lord: in whom you also are built together for a dwelling place of God in the Spirit." (Eph. 2:19-22).

Citizenship has no meaning outside a governmental setting. Just as citizens of dictatorships have no say as to how their lives are governed; those in the kingdom of darkness are slaves to Satan and have no say so in how they are governed.

We, however, are people with liberty. We are no longer slaves of unrighteousness but can choose who we will serve. We are free to live by Faith.

A kingdom has a king and it has citizens. The citizens have rights and privileges because they are in a convent relationship with the king. This is a legal and binding relationship with responsibilities on both parties. The Apostle Paul made mentioned that he was a Roman citizen by birth while others had received their citizenship through purchase. Because he was a citizen, he enjoyed certain privileges.

Just because I am a citizen of the USA does not automatically give me the right to act as an Ambassador. Ambassadors are appointed and therefore, cannot by their own accord, place themselves in that position. Just as importantly, when they are appointed, they are committed to their governments interests and do not speak on their own.

Let us look at the relationship that Jesus had with His Father

- *Jesus said to them, "My Father is always at his work to this very day, and I, too, am working." (John 5:17, NIV)*

- *Jesus gave them this answer: "I tell you the truth, the Son can do nothing by himself; he can do only what he sees his Father doing, because whatever the Father does the Son also does. (John 5:17)*

- *By myself I can do nothing; I judge only as I hear, and my judgment is just, for I seek not to please myself but him who sent me. (John 5:30, NIV)*

- *For I have not spoken on My own authority; but the Father who sent Me gave Me a command, what I should say and what I should speak. And I know that His command is everlasting life. Therefore, whatever I speak, just as the Father has told Me, so I speak." (John 12:49-50)*

What is important for us to see is that Jesus was always doing the will of His Father. As citizens of the Kingdom, doing the will of our Father should be our utmost concern,.

If I am related to the King, does that automatically give to me kingdom powers? No, but it does make it possible for the King to confer upon me special powers to act on his behalf as His delegate. When He calls us to be His Ambassadors, He has confidence in us that we will act on His behalf and do His will.

IX   Health

A healthy nation is a prosperous nation. Sick people cannot work to the best of their ability and contribute to the wealth of the nation. It is more than a matter of economics that moves our King Jesus to provide healing; it is because of His love for those in His kingdom.

It is part of His nature to provide wholeness in body and mind as well as spirit to His people. It is not just because we are God's children that He makes healing available but it is because we are citizens of His Kingdom.

God has made a covenant with the Believer and as part of His kingdom and family; we are entitled to His care and provision. Just as our earthly father watches over our health and provides for us, God does the same for the Believer.

King David tells of the blessings of being connected with God's Kingdom. "Ps 103:2-5, *"Bless the Lord, O my soul, and forget not all His benefits:* *"Who forgives all your iniquities, who heals all your diseases, who redeems your life from destruction, who crowns you with loving-kindness and tender mercies, who satisfies your mouth with good things, so that your youth is renewed like the eagles."*

In the story found in 2 Kings: 5:1-14, Naaman, a beloved general who had contacted leprosy, goes to his master, the King of Syria, who then sends a letter to the King of Israel. When the King of Israel got the letter, he tore his clothes and said, *"Am I God, to kill and make alive, that this man sends a man to me to heal him of his leprosy?"*

The widespread idea was that, since the King of Israel gave out blessings and since healing was in the land of Israel; healing must come from the king. The problem with this thinking was that they were looking to the wrong King. It was the King of Heaven, the true ruler of the Nation of Israel, which provided the healing.

Yes, healing is provided to the citizens; however, even the citizens can receive healing only when two things are present: Trust and Obedience. Both of these are included in the principle of Faith. Trust is a matter of relationship. If you or I trust someone, it is because we believe we know his or her heart or motive. God has no other motive than to show His love for you. Obedience is a result of knowing the Will and the power of the one we are approaching with our request and then doing as He says.

Under the old covenant, God's people were healed when they believed what God said, and then acted on it. Under the new covenant, based on the life, death and resurrection of Jesus, we have even better promises. Jesus fulfilled God's Word and now we have faith that by His stripes we are healed.

Extending the Kingdom of God

We are finding ourselves in kingdom warfare. One culture is trying to dominate another. Jesus, our King, is setting the stage for His return. Before He returns, He is preparing His Church to wage war against the kingdom of darkness. Does this mean spiritual warfare only or does it mean for Kingdom Citizens to rise up within the nations of the world with their voices to oppose those that which would undermine righteousness and justice.

I believe that there are at least five occasions that would allow God's people to rebel against civil authority.

I. A change in government is needed when the culture being created brings great loss to the citizens (loss of freedoms).

II. A rebellion is justified when the self-interests of those governing is at the forefront of their agenda.

III. A rebellion is justified when lawlessness rules the nation.

IV. A rebellion is justified when the very foundational principles that create an orderly society are not only ignored but are also purposely circumvented.

V. A rebellion is justified when those governing are using their influence and power to divide the people to further their ideology and control.

In all that we do, we do it as the Holy Spirit leads us. He provides the plan and strategies to win the battle. Christ is our King and only He has the right to mobilize His troops for various kinds of warfare.

In an orderly society, like the USA, we have the right to voice our concerns and stand up to share our opinions. Let us take our responsibilities seriously and act accordingly.

---

[i] Eagle Forum: "The Phyllis Schlafly Report", Volume 39 #1, 2005, Follies and Failures of the National Education Assn.

Chapter Ten

The Kingdom Established and Lost

Starting at the Beginning

Man is on a journey that leads to God's final purpose for humanity. This journey started at creation and it will continue until Jesus turns everything over to His Father. A lot transpires in between these two events, so it is important that we have a correct starting point.

If we are going to have an understanding of life that allows us to live it to its fullest, we must have a perspective of the whole that sees the very beginning as well as the ending. For this to happen we must begin at the correct starting point and that can only be with God Himself before creation. As with any design, the starting point is within the Creator, within his heart and mind. We must begin with God and see life with a Kingdom mind-set.

We believe in ONE God who reveals Himself as Father, Son, and Holy Spirit. They are equal in all things but with different responsibilities to perform. The overpowering character quality of our Triune God is LOVE and it is out of this LOVE that the unity of the Godhead is seen working together to create the heavens and the Earth. The Father speaks, the Son is the Word spoken and the Spirit (the Spirit of the Father) takes that which the Father speaks and gives it shape and form.

The paternal heart of the Father reveals itself in the creation of the Kingdom of God on earth. It is within this earthly Kingdom that the Father will accomplish four major objectives: *First*, to extend His kingdom from the invisible to the visible and *Secondly*, to make known the fullness of His Being, His full personality. *Thirdly*, His objective is to provide a body of believers for his Son in order that we may share His nature as His children and contribute in the rule of the Kingdom. *Lastly*, it is to provide a temple for the Holy Spirit.

God has a Dream

God is a dreamer and when He dreams, He dreams Big. Big things come from big dreams. God had a Big dream of extending His heavenly, invisible, spiritual kingdom to the visible, earthy and physical realm.

He first sees it as a big puzzle and then he slowly begins to fit all the pieces together. As the pieces come together, he begins to see the picture of something that could be. His dream begins to take shape and form and then He has a vision. God knew it would work because he has all knowledge, understanding and wisdom.

Once He has a vision there is no stopping him. The vision spurs him on to look for all that He needs to make that vision a reality

The Father cannot do it alone so He discusses it with himself (His Word) (also known as self-talk) and with His Spirit. He starts with a conception of that which He is going to create in His mind, in His thoughts.

Regarding earth's kingdom, it is within God first 'unseen' before it was produced (seen). He patterned it after His Kingdom in Heaven and since He cannot change, He must govern this new kingdom in the same fashion using the same righteous standards.

He has a dream of an extended Kingdom that is created in the physical realm with Man having dominion over all His creation. When all his thoughts and plans were finalized, He spoke the Word and the Holy Spirit brought it into existence.

Colonization – Up until recently, schooling in the United States always consisted of World History and American History. Students of my generation were proud to be Americans because we learned of the hardships, struggles and sacrifices that our ancestors endured in order that we might have the society and the life that Americans have enjoyed over the last 200 years.

However, America was not always a sovereign nation. We first were a colony of Great Britain. Great Britain had established a commonwealth of nations and America was destined, at least in their minds, to be a part of that commonwealth. The term Commonwealth originally meant a multiple number of states or nation-states governed for the common good as opposed to an authoritarian state governed for the benefit of a given class of rulers. Great Britain therefore, set out to colonize the new land that was discovered and make it part of their commonwealth.

Other nations also wanted a piece of this land that held so much promise. The Spanish, the French, and others wanted to lay claim to America in order to obtain a share of the great riches that this land had to offer.

The point to be noted is this; before Great Britain started its Colonization there existed no known governmental entity in this great land of ours (except the American Indians). Because it was 'Vacant Land', Great Britain sent people here to incorporate it into their commonwealth. Once a colony had been established, they sent governors to represent the King and an army to insure that this new colony would grow and prosper for the benefit of the commonwealth.

They set up a form of government that gave them control over all things produced, mined, or that otherwise created wealth. They instituted laws, taxes, educational programs, and administrators over water, health and other areas needed for a functioning society. They also influenced this new land with their culture.

Our founding fathers' would have been content to let the King of England rule if he had not tried to take advantage of the fledging colony. When the settlers finally had had enough, they revolted and the United States of America was formed. How did they set up their government? They did not reinvent the wheel regarding governing entirely. They realized that even though they did not want a king to rule over them, they knew they still needed a form of government that would unite the thirteen colonies under one flag, one rule of law that would guarantee the rights of its citizens and a central army whereby they could defend themselves.

They set in place a form of government called a *Republic*. A republic is a form of government in which the head of state is not a monarch and the citizens have an impact on their government. The word 'republic' is derived from the Latin phrase "res publica", which can be translated as "a public affair".[i]

The educational system, of this new republic, used the Bible as their textbook and their national motto was, "One nation under God". The preachers were the watchdogs over what would constitute right and wrong in this ever-growing nation. These preachers, representing God, would preach against the evils of the day until they were silenced or change had occurred. Their preaching affected individuals, families, businesses, education, and government. They, in reality, were like the Old Testament Prophets who made the Word of God known when the people and their kings strayed or departed from the LAW.

The Lord's Prayer – During what we refer to as the Sermon on the Mount, Jesus addresses the crowd and tells them plainly that He is the Son of God. He does so by addressing God as "Our Father" in what we call, The Lord's Prayer. He means to emphasis the fact that His Father is in Heaven and as such, He is to be worshipped. Jesus then begins his prayer and the first thing that He asks is for the Father's Kingdom to come and His will to be done here on earth as it is in Heaven.

Jesus wanted the government of His Father's kingdom to return to earth. When His Father's Kingdom was ruling the earth, there was no sickness, no poverty, no pain, and no death. Jesus asks for the provision to be granted to his disciples and for forgiveness to be sought and for the Father to keep them from temptation in order that his disciples would be able to exercise authority over Satan and his demons. The Kingdom of God was the true Kingdom or government of the earth and one day His Kingdom will have power and the glory over the earth forever and forever.

The Creation of Man

Man was made in God's Image – OT: Hebrew: demuwth (dem- ooth'); Spirit.

To be made in the *image* of another is to be made exactly like the original or have the same nature as the original. The Image is hidden or invisible but is expressed by the actions, attitudes and feelings. The image is the character of the original. Man was made in the image of his Creator. Man was created to express God's character or nature.

God is a Spirit, therefore to be made in God's image means to also be a spirit being. It is through Spirit to spirit communication that God intended for Man to exercise dominion over the earth as His representative.

Man was made after God's Likeness – OT: Hebrew: tselem (tseh'lem); Soul

To be made after the *likeness* of another is to behave in *the same* manner and express the same purpose of exsistance as another. Likeness is outward; it is the behavior and actions that are seen. It is more than just being a loyal and faithful representative of God, it is to go about our assignment (operate and function) in the same manner as did our Creator.

IF GOD DID NOT CREATE THE EARTH, HE COULD NOT JUSTIFY CREATING MAN IN HIS IMAGE. WHY? GOD'S NATURE DEMANDS THAT HE EXERCISE DOMINION OVER ALL THAT HE POSSESSES. IF HE HAD CREATED MAN TO OCCUPY HEAVEN, HE COULD NOT HAVE MADE HIM IN HIS IMAGE BECAUSE GOD WILL NOT SHARE HIS GLORY WITH ANY OF THOSE HE HAS CREATED. THEREFORE, HE CREATED EARTH AND THEN MAN, THAT HE MIGHT HAVE DOMINION IN THE PHYSICAL REALM.

Before Adam rebelled, he was righteous and holy. He communed with His Creator and was faithful and obedient in all that he was given to do. He was given all the resources necessary to carry out his responsibilities of tending the garden and naming the animals. He was submissive to His Creator.

God said, "Let them have dominion". The, "them" refers to Adam and his wife and ALL their offspring. When God breathed life into man, there was, at that moment, a transfer of power. God delegates the responsibility, management and rule of His Kingdom to man. It is important that we understand the two terms used when God created man; image and likeness.

We hear many say today that we are created in the image of God, as if Man today is like His creator. This is not true. When Adam and Eve rebelled against God, his spirit died within him and only faith in God's promise and obedience to His commandments restored or renewed his spirit. So it is the same today. Only faith and obedience renews our spirit and enables us to have Spirit to spirit communication as at the beginning. From there we must go on to maturity.

The end of Man's Dominion

God had given them one command; *"Of every tree of the garden you may freely eat; but of the tree of the knowledge of good and evil you shall not eat, for in the day that you eat of it you shall surely die. Gen 2:17.*

God had given them a conscience and a free will but Satan blinded their spiritual eyes to see the consequences to what they were about to do. They were about to believe the biggest lie ever told, "You don't need Spirit to spirit communication in order to have dominion over the earth. There's a tree, right over there, which will provide all the knowledge, understanding and wisdom you need. God is keeping it from you but you can take a bite from that tree's fruit and it and ALL will be yours."

Adam had given the snake its name and found nothing in it or in the garden that would hurt him or cause him or his wife any harm. So when the snake spoke to Eve, she did not become alarmed or afraid, although it was unusual for a snake or an animal to speak. Even though Adam and Eve enjoyed perfect communion with the Father, they allowed a snake to deceive them.

Obedience was the key to receive blessing for Adam and Eve and it is still that way for us today. When he rebelled, he lost the right to rule God's kingdom here on earth. He lost his ability to have dominion and rule because he lost his Spirit to spirit communication. Without this communication, he was in a state of confusion, not knowing right from wrong. He forgot this very important lesson; Obedience brings the blessing.

Before Creation

In order that we might fully understand how the Kingdom was lost, we have to go back before the creation of the heavens and the earth. We have to go back to eternity past and look into the Kingdom of Heaven. We need to see what happened there that would eventually have a direct effect on Man's dominion of the earth.

The Bible itself gives us a picture of the Kingdom of Heaven: *"Your throne, O God, is forever and ever; a scepter of righteousness is the scepter of Your kingdom. You love righteousness and hate wickedness."* (Ps 45:6-7).

God created all things; therefore, Lucifer, an angel, is a created being even though the Bible says he was more beautiful (a gem among precious stones, Ezekiel. 28:13-17) than all the others. Lucifer had access to God's presence as the worship leader of Heaven, nevertheless when pride entered his heart Lucifer knew exactly what he wanted and how he was going to get it. Listen to the five "I will's" statements from Isaiah 14:12-15 that he proudly boast:

I will ascend into Heaven

I will exalt my throne

I will also sit on the mount

I will ascend above the heights of the clouds

I will be like the most High

Lucifer was determined to go after what only God the Creator possessed-glory, honor, dominion and power. What Satan failed to understand was that: God will not share His Glory with anyone. Neither will He share His Kingdom with anyone except His only begotten Son and with those that will be joint heirs with Him.

Because of his deception, God changed his name from Lucifer to Satan and he was expelled from God's Kingdom in Heaven. The Word of God does not leave us ignorant of who Satan is and who he has become. He is the Deceiver, the father of all lies, the ruler of Darkness and the enemy of God.

Satan's Plan to get a Kingdom

Satan's plan to obtain a kingdom was to deceive Mankind just as he had deceived the angels that had fallen with him. He would promise them that they would be like God themselves. He knew, from experience, that when humanity rebelled, God would have no choice but to expel them from the garden and from His presence just as God had expelled him.

Once done, he would take over as ruler and step number one would be complete; Satan would have a kingdom. Satan would organize his kingdom after the pattern in heaven. He would copy God's organizational structure. Satan seeks to copy everything that God has and everything He has done. Satan did not create anything; he has only copied God's work and then perverted it to his own use.

Satan organized his demons (fallen angels) just as God has organized his angels. We see in Colossians 1:16 the pattern as *God created all things, visible and invisible, whether thrones or dominions or principalities or powers.* The same again in Ephesians 6:12, we see that *we do not wrestle against flesh and blood but against; principalities, against powers, against the rulers of the darkness of this age, against spiritual hosts of wickedness in heavenly places.*

THE KINGDOM LOST

37

Satan's kingdom is this world. He and his demons tempt, deceive, oppress in order to bring people into the bondage of fear so that they can control them and take away their freedom. His kingdom is governed by a system of beliefs that are contrary to the Word of God. His worldly kingdom influences art, music, politics, spiritual matters, science, philosophy and all other aspects of life contrived without God. We are born into this world and under Satan's control until we are 'born again'.

Satan heard the Promise given to Adam but realizes that if he could deceive humanity into accepting a perverted view of what an acceptable worldview should be, he could prevent his kingdom from being destroyed. Without God's people holding up the light of truth, the world is deceived and millions of people will face the same fate as that of Satan and his demons.

Satan's plan is to obliterate the message of the Kingdom of God and replace it with a moral belief system; a system that puts man at the center instead of God. Satan leaves in enough truth to make it reasonable, but his substitute is full of corruption.

The Kingdom Understood

There is nothing more important to the Church today than a clear concise understanding of the Kingdom of God. Jesus calls everyone to repentance: meaning to have a change in their thinking. Therefore, He spends much time explaining what is offered in place of what they are now holding on to. The Jews were holding on to a false idea of the Kingdom and obedience to the Law as the means to please God.

Given that our destiny is tied to the Kingdom of God, we must recognize six things that Satan does not want you to know:

- The Kingdom of God is available for you to enter, now

- How to enter the Kingdom

- Once you enter the Kingdom of God, you are a citizen

- There is a distinct culture in the Kingdom of God

- You have authority in the Kingdom of God

- There is power available through the Baptism in the Holy Spirit to overcome the enemy

Different Kingdoms

The terms, the Kingdom of Heaven and the Kingdom of God are both used in the Gospels, therefore, the first thing that needs to be addressed is the question; is there a difference between these two terms. Both belong to the spiritual realm but is there a difference?

The Kingdom of Heaven is the sphere or jurisdiction where the Father rules over all creation, including the Heavenlies. His authority is exercised over his entire domain. It is here that His throne is established. Before the foundations of the earth and the heavens, Jesus existed as the Father's Word. There was only one throne and this was the governmental center in the spiritual realm where the Father executed judgment as well as mercy and grace over His Kingdom. All beings, whether Angels, Cherubs, Arch Angels, Seraphim and Cherubim, are subject to His demands and both His authority and power are absolute.

However, when His Word took on flesh and became a man, the Father started to rearrange the furniture in the throne room. Jesus was obedient to all that He was given to do (He took upon himself the sins of the whole world and paid the penalty of death to satisfy the judgment of God). Because of His obedience, the Father has given Him a name above of all names. When Jesus ascended into Heaven after being on the earth 40 days after His resurrection from the dead, God made Him His Lord and Christ and set Him upon His own throne from which He will judge those that are alive and the dead.

Jesus is subject to His father's authority and even though He will one day rule as King of kings and Lord of lords, He too, does the will of the Father. When we talk about Jesus being King of kings, we are talking of governments. When we are talking about Jesus being Lord of lords we are talking of ownership of property.

The Kingdom of God is also a spiritual kingdom but there are two big differences. The first difference is the sphere of influence. The jurisdiction of the Kingdom of God is not in the heavenlies but in the hearts of men on the earth. The second difference is the person in the position of authority. Jesus is the King of this earth and His Father has given all authority to Him. Jesus is King but not all peoples of the earth are His subjects. His jurisdiction is restricted to those that are Citizens of the Kingdom; it is to the Believers that He gives permission to use His authority to act as His representatives.

The Father sent His Word, clothed in flesh, and because we believe His Word, the Father has given us power to become His children. Throughout the Gospels, Jesus gave a clear picture of His Kingdom and what would be expected of the citizens of His Kingdom. The Father took us out from the kingdom of darkness and translated us into Kingdom of His Son. By His Spirit, we are "born again" and therefore He said that if we give ourselves as a living sacrifice, we would be transformed into the image of His Son. When completed, God's Grand Plan would be realized.

As citizens of the Kingdom of God, we are also citizens of the Kingdom of Heaven. I have never been to Heaven (except in the spirit-Heb 4:16) but I am very much a part of the Kingdom of Heaven as that is where my Father resides and has His throne. The authority that the Father gave to His Son, His Son has given to us that we might go and extend His Kingdom – the Kingdom of God throughout the whole earth.

---

[i] http://en.wikipedia.org/wik/Republic

Chapter Eleven

The Kingdom Reclaimed

God sets His plan into motion

Before God could fulfill His Grand Plan for us, He had to reclaim His Kingdom from the usurper, Satan himself. Satan stole His Kingdom from those He had personally put in charge to establish His rule here on earth. Therefore, God began His own spiritual warfare against Satan. This fight was between two kingdoms, between two governments.

So the Lord God said to the serpent, "This is your punishment: You are singled out from among all the domestic and wild animals of the whole earth-to be cursed. You shall gravel in the dust as long as you live, crawling along on your belly. From now on, you and the woman will be enemies, as will your offspring and hers. You will strike his heel, but he will crush your head."

The first part of this pronouncement deals with the snake, who allowed himself to be used to deceive man. The serpent was subject to Adam because God had given Adam DOMINION over the creatures on the earth and the fishes of the sea. Therefore, by agreeing to be an instrument in the deception of Eve, a curse fell upon it. Whatever form it once occupied, the serpent is now to crawl upon its belly and swallow the dust of the earth.

God pronounced the curse to the serpent and then gives the first prophecy of a deathblow to Satan's deceitfully acquired kingdom. God is declaring that He will provide a deliverer who will reclaim His kingdom. This God does in the hearing of Adam and Eve that they might know that they can be forgiven and that it will provide them hope for the future.

The second pronouncement is a Promise. Their faith in the God of the Promise will restore them back into a relationship where peace within will abound. It is a short statement but it speaks volumes.

The Promise is in vague terms and has a quality of mystery and vagueness, therefore it is difficult to understand or interpret. There are no particulars such as; mode of deliverance, the time it is to come, or the agency by which it is to come. This should not surprise us as the Bible is written to believers and requires revelation from the one who inspired men to write it, the Holy Spirit. It does not require a college education or high intelligence; it only requires a humble spirit that is alive to the voice of God.

The Promise

With this Promise, God is saying, "Even though Satan has achieved his first objective of acquiring a kingdom; my Son will in the end, destroy his kingdom. Satan will think he has won over the opposition when he provokes men to kill Jesus. However, Jesus will be resurrected and He will win the victory over death and the grave."

War is declared between the seed of Satan (the children of disobedience) and the seed of the woman, Jesus. The hope of the world is contained in this Promise; a Promise that a future descendant of Adam would again have dominion over the earth.

Everything that follows in recorded history is documentation of this war between Satan's warriors and God's men of faith. We hear of people like Enoch, Noah, Abraham and Sarah and the Patriarchs. Everything relates to this Promise of reclaiming the Kingdom that was lost. It was not man that was lost; it was his kingdom. Reclaim the kingdom and in the process, man will be restored to fellowship with God.

In this Promise, God's people would see the mercy and grace of their Creator. It is a mercy and grace of such magnitude that it restores man to a place of purpose and fulfillment. Nevertheless, the only thing that would allow this Promise to be realized is a change in government.

Suppressive governments take away; steal all dignity and self-respect that is instinctive in each man. I saw for myself, in communist Poland and in Myanmar that people living under Communism and Socialism or under dictatorships of self-centered men know firsthand the horror of such action. They feel worthless and of no value, therefore, their morals decline and their cultures decline with them.

Adam, because he had lived under the government of God, knew immediately what had happened when he rebelled. He saw the shift in rulership from a benevolent God to a ruthless dictator.

God, in order that man would know that He keeps His promise, entered into covenants that would bind the two of them together. Man could rely on God to fulfill His promise because a relationship was established.

God's Prophecies of Reclaiming His Kingdom

God kept His promise alive by raising up prophets to reveal His strategy. Here is the strategy: He would provide a Messiah who would be a future King whose kingdom would have no end. God gave the promise to Adam and it was passed on from individual to individual until God found a man and woman who had faith in the promise that would exceed their sight of old age and their inability to have children. This couple would be the root beginnings of a family of Hebrew children and later a nation. His name was Abraham and to him the promise became more specific because it was from his seed, that the promised Messiah would come and all the nations would be blessed.

So from that time forward, prophets were chosen from among men to proclaim that God would keep His Promise. Until the time of Christ's birth, God's strategy was to give to Man more and more revelation as to who His Messiah would be. Let us look at some of these prophecies:

- *"For unto us a Child is born, Unto us a Son is given; And the government will be upon His shoulder. And His name will be called Wonderful, Counselor, Mighty God, Everlasting Father, Prince of Peace. Of the increase of His government and peace there will be no end, upon the throne of David and over His kingdom, to order it and establish it with judgment and justice from that time forward, even forever."* (Isa. 9:6-7)

- *"I was watching in the night visions, And behold, One like the Son of Man, Coming with the clouds of heaven! He came to the Ancient of Days, And they brought Him near before Him. Then to Him was given dominion, glory, and a kingdom that all peoples, nations, and languages should serve Him. His dominion is an everlasting dominion, which shall not pass away, And His kingdom the one which shall not be destroyed."* (Dan. 7:13-14)

The Promise Fulfilled

God reclaimed his Kingdom just as was prophesied 4000 years earlier. In the fullness of time, Jesus was born of a virgin and as promised He re-established His Father's kingdom through His sinless life, veracious death on the cross, resurrection, and then finally His ascension unto the right hand of the Father.

Satan's power over man is now broken and Christ takes back the keys of the kingdom. The power of sin is broken although Satan's head is not crushed. This will take place after the battle of Armageddon.

Jesus was fulfilling the Promise given to Adam. The Father knew how He was going to reclaim His kingdom and the virgin birth of His Son was the beginning of that fulfillment. *"Since by one man sin came into the world, it is by one man that sin would be taken away. Jesus lived a sinless life before all the people, took upon himself the sin of all mankind, and bore the*

105

curse for all; that ALL may be set free". He made an open display of all his enemies and conquered the grave when the Father raised Him from the dead. When He accomplished all that He was given to do, He sat down at the right hand of His Father. When He fulfilled His purpose, our Father made him both his Lord and His Christ to sit upon His throne.

Christ's disciples enjoy the many blessings that come along with Jesus reclaiming His Father's Kingdom. Among them, Jesus gives to His disciples New Life. He gives them power to become children of God and enjoy a personal relationship with Him. Jesus' resurrection began the re-establishment of the Kingdom of God, and the returning to Man his place of dominion. Jesus destroyed the power of sin by paying the penalty of rebellion against His Father, therefore, man is now free to choose whom he will serve.

We can look at what Jesus has done but it is important to note why he did what he did. Paul writes in Galatians 4:4-5, *"But when the fullness of the time had come, God sent forth His Son, born of a woman, born under the law, to redeem those who were under the law, that we might receive the adoption as sons.* See more on this important subject of Adoption in Chapter 15.

Within the action of God's reclaiming His Kingdom, two major events took place. They are now part of Church doctrine and must be understood by all who claim to be Christian: Redemption and Justification.

Redemption - Free to Serve God

In order for us to understand God's method of restoring Man to his original position of having dominion, we need to go back to the Old Testament and see the covenant that He made with Abraham, Isaac and Jacob. God promises Abraham that He would multiply his descendants and give the land of Canaan to be theirs, forever. God promises to make Abraham's descendants numerous and to bless all nations through them. God's promise is passed down to his grandson, Jacob. Jacob has twelve sons and this is where we pick up the story in Genesis 28-50.

When we come to the end of the story of Joseph, we see Israel's descendants under slavery in the land of Egypt. Just as Abraham had prophesied, his descendants were in bondage for 400 years and then it was time for God to bring His favored people out and establish them in their own land, 'The Promised Land'.

In God's timing, He raises up a leader, Moses, from His people. This Moses undergoes a time of preparation, 40 years in exile, until he is made ready to be God's deliverer and do things according to God's plan.

When Moses finally realizes, that it is only God's supernatural power that will bring release to the Hebrew people, God sends him back to face the most powerful man on the planet at that time, Pharaoh. Through a series of ten supernatural acts, Pharaoh is forced to let the Hebrew people go. However, their redemption is not complete until God does one additional supernatural act through his servant Moses. He orders Moses to take the Rod that he has in his hand and strike the waters of the Red Sea, allowing the Hebrew people to cross over on dry ground. When it is all over, several million descendants of Jacob are redeemed from slavery and Pharaoh is killed in the returning waters.

This is a beautiful picture of God's love for His chosen people and of His faithfulness to His covenant with Abraham, Isaac and Jacob. However, there is more to the story than that.

This is the point to know and understand; God was not just bringing a people out of bondage but He was taking unto Himself a people with which He will have a relationship. He says, *"I am Yahweh... I will free you from slavery... and I will take you for my people and I will be your God"*. In virtue of the covenant, Israel becomes a "holy people", consecrated to God.

What had happened was more than physical; it was also spiritual. There is a union established between God and the Hebrew people. Since God is a Spirit and Man is a spirit, God is allowing them to come into a relationship where they can talk with Him and He with them. It is a relationship where they can again receive knowledge, understanding and wisdom.

God does not come in by force and just take the Hebrew people from Pharaoh; He demands that a price be paid for their enslavement;. This is a story of redemption of something that belonged to someone else. This, however is not a commercial transaction regulated by the law of equality, where the jailer will free a prisoner or the merchant will sell his merchandise only on the condition that he suffers no loss. It is about a justice to be carried out and that justice was going to fall on the Egyptians.

It is a story about God fulfilling His covenant with the Hebrew people and about the Egyptian people who held them captive. Blood was the price for the Hebrew people, therefore the Egyptians, in the end, were going to shed the blood of their first-born.

In Exodus 4:2-3, Moses lets us know that God, for the first time, is making Himself known to the Hebrew children as Lord. This name,

Lord, denotes Ownership. Therefore, when He redeems them from Pharaoh, He is claiming something that belongs to Him as the Owner.

God entered into a covenant with them and established it with His Word. Their part was to offer a pure lamb as a sacrifice for their sin, which would keep them in good standing.

When God brought them forth, He made them into a nation with a ruler over them, which did not exist up until that time. That ruler was to be God Himself. They were no longer going to be known as the Hebrew people or the people of Israel (Jacob's name had been changed by God to Israel), they would be known as the nation of Israel.

As a nation, they were to have a structure of laws and statues to keep order and peace within their society. They were to be a 'holy' people unto Him and they would be known to other nations as having an almighty God that watched over His people. Because of their obedience to the Laws that governed their life style, other nations would see that their culture was the reason for them being a blessed people.

Although the Nation of Israel did not follow the laws of their God for very long, He did not forsake them. He did send other nations to punish them but He never forsook them, why, because the redemption story goes far beyond the beginnings of the nation of Israel at the Red Sea.

When the kingdom of David was divided, God raised up Prophets that kept the promise of redemption alive. There was to be a future redemption for the nation of Israel. There was a promise that another 'deliverer' would come forth from the loins of the Nation of Judah. A messiah would come forth that would deliver his people from the very power of sin that kept them from keeping the Law that was given to them through Moses.

King David writes in Ps. 130:7, 8, *"O Israel, hope in the Lord; For with the Lord there is mercy, And with Him is abundant redemption. And He shall redeem Israel from all his iniquities".*

In Jer 31:31, 32, *"Behold, the days are coming, says the Lord, when I will make a new covenant with the house of Israel and with the house of Judah — not according to the covenant that I made with their fathers in the day that I took them by the hand to lead them out of the land of Egypt, My covenant which they broke, though I was a husband to them, says the Lord".*

This covenant will be unlike the previous covenant. God's own Messiah would come on the scene to bring the Hebrew people a new covenant, along with a kingdom that will have no end. It will not be a new kingdom but a reclaiming of the original kingdom, the kingdom of God.

The exciting thing about this new covenant is that God said, through His Prophet Ezekiel, *"I will put my spirit in you"*. This makes it possible for those who receive this new covenant to have direct communication with God. He makes this 'New Covenant' also available to the Gentiles through the way of 'Faith'.

Although God opens the door to the Gentiles, He has not forgotten the Nation of Israel; He will continue His redemption story regarding them at the end of the age.

This story of deliverance of the Hebrew people is a picture of our deliverance from sin. The Messiah, who was born, died and rose again from the dead, is the beginning of our redemption story. When we are 'Born Again', we are redeemed. Our slavery was just as real as the Children of Israel's slavery under the hand of the Egyptians, only theirs was physical and ours is spiritual. God has freed us from the penalty of sin. He has freed us from the power that sin had in our life. Just as justice demanded a payment from the Egyptians (the death of their first-born), our Redemption also required a payment and that payment was the blood of Jesus Christ, God's first-born Son; *"for without the shedding of blood there is no remission of sin."*

As part of the Adamic race, man is under the dominion of Satan. All those born of women are children of disobedience and are influenced by his lies, deceit and desire to destroy all that is righteous in this world. But thanks be unto God, we have been delivered out of the kingdom of darkness and "translated" into the kingdom of the Son.

Jesus' purpose, mission, and desire was and is to return to God His creation clothed in righteousness; including man. To know that we are restored into His presence is the source of our joy. There is no greater outward expression of those that call themselves children of God then that of joy. No one else can have it and no one can steal it from us. It is spiritual in its making. It is ours because we are redeemed and in fellowship with our Creator.

Reconciliation, reunion with God

Contained in the story of Redemption is the thought of Reconciliation. Redemption speaks of the wrath of God, which is now removed. Reconciliation speaks to the relationship with God that is restored.

When God created Man, He gave to him a spirit that enabled communication between heaven and earth. This pathway of Spirit to spirit communication allowed God to bring to Man the knowledge, understanding and wisdom needed for Man to have dominion over the earth. It was and is essential for Man to maintain this pathway or else chaos, confusion, and turmoil will be the result.

Satan offered Man an alternative pathway; one that allowed him freedom from the work of maintaining the relationship with his creator. He offered him the fruit from the tree of knowledge of good and evil. All he had to do was 'pick and eat'. It sounded so simple and easy as compared to always having to go to God when he needed knowledge, understanding or wisdom.

When God redeemed Man from the penalty for his sin, He also renewed his spirit so that he could again have Spirit to spirit communication. This communication is what allowed or enabled Man to have dominion over the earth.

When we put our faith and trust in Jesus Christ, the blood of Jesus does not only redeem us but the blood brings us close to the heart of God the Father. Christ's blood gives us power to become God's children, therefore, we can use Christ's name in all our dealings with Him.

We are a new creation with a new heart; therefore, we can approach His throne whenever we have a need for mercy or grace. Our Father is always open to hear from us whether it is to hear a request or our thanks and praise or our confession of sin.

Justification - Born Again and now Citizens

Every person wants to feel that he or she has importance and does not deserve condemnation. We all want to be justified in our thoughts, words and deeds. We all want to stand in the face of our accusers and be able to say, "I told you, it's OK what I did". We all want to declare our "righteousness. We feel justified when we can make our cause triumph over that of an opponent and make the justice of our case known. Here is a problem; God says our Righteousness is as filthy rags.

One word characterizes the Kingdom of God: Righteousness. The scepter that is in the King's right hand is Righteousness. The foundation of God's throne is Righteousness and Justice. However, the one word that characterizes Satan's kingdom or the kingdoms of this world is the complete opposite and that word is lawlessness.

When we consider our ways, have a change in our thinking regarding our sinfulness and seek God for forgiveness, God declares us

110

justified or that justice has been satisfied. We receive this "declaration" by faith.

So here is the **FIRST** aspect of Justification; When Satan comes to accuse us before our Father, we hold in our hand a statement from God that says that we are justified or that justice has been served. Therefore, we can 'live by faith'. This has HUGE implications for us.

SECONDLY, through Justification, we come boldly before the throne of God to receive mercy and grace in our time of need. Justification places Man back into a position of "right standing", therefore, we can stand before God without the threat of punishment because we now stand before Him, clothed in the righteousness of Christ. It is in consideration of this word, Justification, that we understand the justice and the holiness of God.

This aspect of Justification is so important because we can now come before the throne and make our petitions before the Living God. In James 5:16 we have it written, *"The effective, fervent prayer of a righteous man avails much"*. It is the righteous man that pleads for the souls of the lost, healing for the sick, and deliverance for those captive and receives answers.

When God's people embrace this aspect of Justification, God rejoices. It is in knowing that they are justified that cause His followers to go out into the fields and make His name known to the ungodly and bring Righteousness to the Earth. It is in so doing that God's people are involved in extending His Kingdom throughout the whole Earth.

The **THIRD** aspect is so very important for us to consider. When the father (in Luke 15:11-32) saw his prodigal son return, his heart leaped for joy. The son who was lost is now found. He calls for a robe to be put on him, a ring to be put on his finger and sandals to be placed on his feet. The father was restoring his son to a place of importance in His kingdom as a citizen.

The father showed his son more than mercy; he showed him grace. The father by his actions granted his son justification. We, who by our faith in Christ have received the gift of Redemption and this abundance of grace, will now reign in life through Jesus Christ.

Those that do not have a Kingdom mindset overlook this very important part of Justification. This restoration to our original position before God allows us to take up again our role of Regent for the King of Heaven.

The **FOURTH** aspect of Justification is - eradication of our sinful nature. The old saying for the meaning of Justification, "Just as if we didn't sin" is true, old things have passed away and all things have become new. God takes away our stony heart and replaces it with a heart of flesh so that we may walk in His statutes and keep his judgments. Therefore, God is not ashamed to call us His people and He will be our God.

If we still have a sinful nature, how could God ever say to us, "be perfect for I am perfect" and "be holy for I am holy"? We can no longer hide behind those familiar sayings, "I am not perfect, just forgiven" or "I'm just a sinner saved by grace". God will not accept such frivolous concoctions of the flesh - to save the flesh.

However, herein lies the problem for the Believer; the flesh is still subject to the influence of evil. Within our flesh, there is no good thing. It is only as we put to death our flesh in all areas of our lives that the Holy Spirit can transform us into the very image of Jesus Christ.

There is also the **FIFTH** aspect of Justification that comes with the gift of righteousness. It is this: Since God has given us a new spirit, God does not deal with our spirit nature any longer as an enemy. He now deals with our flesh. The flesh is the recipient of Satan's offensive moves against us. When we sin, it is not because of our sinful nature; the heart of flesh replaced that. When we sin, it is through our flesh. That is why we don't have to be "Born Again" every time we sin. We just need to confess our sin, *"and He is faithful and just to forgive us our sins and cleanse us from all unrighteousness"*.

For this reason, demons can also cast out from people. demons do not inhabit our spirit but they can oppress our flesh. This is the explanation as to why a spirit can oppress Christians and why we can cast them out.

In summary, Justification for God means that He now has a people who He can make ready to rule in His place and that He can now precede with His Grand Plan for His creation.

The Pharisees of Jesus' day believed that if they obeyed God's Law they would be justified. In fact, if they could accomplish this, then they really would be justified. However, the Pharisees made an error in their understanding of the covenant. They separated the Law from the Promise where Faith is required.

Let us look at Justification as involving two kingdoms. Jesus' mission was and is to provide a way for man to be restored to the relationship he had with God and to restore righteousness to the Earth.

His purpose involves restoring Man back to the position that he had before Satan deceived him.

Adam received his authority, from God his Creator, the ruler of the heavenly Kingdom. It was because of his relationship with the Creator that God gave him dominion over the Earth. He had both – Relationship and Position. When Adam rebelled against God, he lost both.

When Jesus invaded the realm of Satan, He conquered and destroyed his power over Man. By His death, resurrection and ascension He accomplished the reclaiming of His Father's kingdom. This would be meaningless, however, unless He also provided a way for Man to be restored to a position where-by he could take dominion over the earth as God originally intended.

Man receives this justification by Faith. It is only by Faith that he is justified.

These two important truths of Redemption and Justification cannot be overlooked or ignored. Every "Born Again" believer must understand these terms and have them imbedded in their heart and mind. These are spiritual truths and they can only be lived out in the Believer by revelation that comes by the Holy Spirit.

SALVATION INCORPORATES BOTH REDEMPTION AND JUSTIFICATION. IT HOW THEY FIT INTO OUR WORLDVIEW, HOWEVER, THAT DETERMINES WHETHER WE WILL HAVE A BIBLICAL MAN-CENTERED OR A KINGDOM WORLDVIEW.

Until Christians understand the full meaning of Redemption and Justification, they will never advance toward God's Grand Plan. Until the Kingdom is re-established, the Grand Plan of the Father can never be realized. God gave Man dominion over the earth to rule it and take care of it, therefore the Church must make known and keep these two doctrines in remembrance to the Church.

Chapter Twelve

The Kingdom Re-Established

It's Ours

Paul's student, Epaphras who had been converted in Ephesus, returned home to Colossae to proclaim the gospel and as a result the Church is born in that city. Paul writes to the Church in Colossae and he can hardly contain himself. He has heard of their faith and the love they have toward the saints. He prays for them that they might be filled with the knowledge of His will in all wisdom and spiritual understanding in order that they may walk worthy of the Lord, fully pleasing Him, being fruitful in every good work and increasing in the knowledge of God.

What he is excited about is this; they received deliverance from the power of darkness and found a new way of living in the Kingdom of the Son of God. He is excited because now the kingdom and its culture will be established in their lives and when seen and desired by others, the Kingdom of God will be extended.

A kingdom finds expression through its culture. Kingdom culture will find it expression in the heart of the believer, in his home, in his business, in the school, in the local church, and in the local, county, state and national governments. Those living in the world will see the difference. This will awaken and excite their desire and allow the Holy Spirit opportunity to speak to their hearts.

When the Apostles went to a city, they proclaimed the Gospel of the Kingdom and then allowed the Holy Spirit to confirm the truth of their words with signs and wonders, healings and the casting out of demons.

The Kingdom of God is confirmed but it is not extended because of supernatural activity. The kingdom is extended as people live-out the culture of the Kingdom on a day to day basis. This is the real proof that Jesus has re-established His Kingdom and is still alive as King of the Kingdom.

"The Kingdom of God is at hand"

Jesus demonstrates throughout his earthly ministry that the Kingdom of God with all of its power had come; demons are cast out, the lame walk, the blind see and the deaf hear. Jesus sent out His 12 and His 70 and gave them the same power He possessed. This He did to show that the Kingdom was not just in Him but that His word was true when He said, *"The Kingdom of God is within you"*.

If supernatural acts were all Jesus did, He would not have re-established His Father's kingdom, because a kingdom needs citizens and territory as well as a King. He calls for people to follow Him and willingly become His disciples. In His prayer to His Father, He speaks of these new citizens, *"Now I am no longer in the world, but these are in the world, and I come to You. Holy Father, keep through Your name those whom You have given Me, that they may be one as We are . While I was with them in the world, I kept them in Your name. Those whom You gave Me I have kept;* ...John 17:11-12

If He was going to influence his citizens, He needed to institute a culture that they could accept and live-out. This, Jesus did through His teaching and preaching throughout His ministry. The Sermon on the Mount is a capsule and the essence of what He taught.

Jesus was able to re-claim the Kingdom of God by satisfying the justice of God and by taking away the Keys to the Kingdom from Satan. These keys He now gives to His Church to extend His kingdom.

When Paul writes to the Church at Corinth, he makes it clear that he does not need letters of recommendation because they were his written epistles, read by all men; clearly, they were an epistle of Christ, written not by ink but by the Holy Spirit.

When writing to the Church at Thessalonica, he gives thanks to God for their work of faith, labor of love and patience of hope. He says his gospel did not come in word only but also in much power and in the Holy Spirit.

I can just see Jesus looking down at these two Churches and saying with great emotion, "NOW, That's what I'm talking about. That's Kingdom Living".

The Timing of the Kingdom

The problem for the Church today is that we are thinking like disciples instead of citizens. We are trying to be disciples by trying 'to be like Jesus' through what we do (WWJD), instead of allowing the Holy Spirit to transform us. We are told that we are to (reflect) the image of Jesus; when in fact we are to be transformed into His image and unto His likeness.

The motive for our Christian work seems to be to populate heaven with God-like people instead of extending His Kingdom. We teach how to be a 'better you' instead of teaching how to live-out Kingdom culture for the world to see. When the world sees Kingdom Culture then they will know that the King of glory is alive.

You were born for a purpose just as Jesus was born for a purpose. Jesus, in fulfilling His purpose to restore Righteousness to the earth, died, rose again and ascended. It is our purpose to extend the Father's Kingdom so that Righteousness is restored to the earth.

Some would say that the Kingdom of God is for the future. So is the Kingdom of God for the Future only or has Jesus come to set up His kingdom now? Matthew tells us, *"After John was put in prison, Jesus came to Galilee, preaching the gospel of the kingdom of God, and saying, "The time is fulfilled, and the kingdom of God is at hand. Repent, and believe in the gospel."* Jesus also said, *"The Kingdom of God is within you."* He taught His disciples to pray saying, *"Our Father hallowed be thy name, thy kingdom come on earth as it is in heaven..."* Is He saying; it is now as well as future?

It is significant to know therefore, that the Kingdom is present and it is future. If we believe the Kingdom of God is only for the future, we must accept Predeterminism as the underpinning of our Faith. With this belief, we are left with the somber thought that our Creator is Sovereign and therefore, will do whatever-whenever, as he sees fit.

Because the Kingdom of God is now, Jesus has given to His disciples (citizens) the responsibility to continue to spread the Word that the King has come. We are to be His Ambassadors.

The Word Ambassador has no meaning if there is no kingdom. Just because his Kingdom is not of this world, it does not mean that it has not come. It is a spiritual kingdom but it is more real than the kingdoms of this world. His kingdom will stand forever while the kingdoms of this world will pass away.

Luke, the writer of the Book of Acts, tells us that when Peter got up to address the Jews he said, *"Therefore let all the house of Israel know assuredly that God has made this Jesus, whom you crucified, both Lord and Christ."* The Jews that heard Peter understood exactly what he meant; Jesus came to set up His kingdom, not physically but spiritually and they responded accordingly.

Satan has deceived even the "called out ones" and has caused many to think the Kingdom of God is for the future only. By his deception, he has kept the Church from advancing. If the Church had advanced, she would have dismantled his kingdom little by little. Because of his deception, however, there has been no opposition and Satan's kingdom has increased year after year.

We are now at a time, when all gains that have been made for the advancement of the Kingdom of God seem small in comparison. We are living at a time when many claim to be Christian, but as we look at the tree, there is no fruit. There is no faith for the miraculous, no room for the supernatural to be played out in their lives.

The Church's Future

In the study of church and secular history, we can note the changes that have taken place. Sometimes these changes were predictable and at other times, they were not. Predictable change is comfortable. It is comfortable because it comes because of cycles or foreknowledge and therefore allows for some degree of control. When we can control change, it does not control us and we just continue from the present into the future.

When change appears to be cyclical, as it has been in the past, we should stop and take note and see if it justifies making a prediction for the future. In this case, I believe it does. Struss and Howe, in their 1991 book, *Generations*, pointed out two pivotal points that represent a significant moment in the collective social life in our culture.[i] These pivotal points influence what is felt before and after them for about ten years. They have called these two points, a spiritual awakening and a secular crisis. In between these two points, they have discerned two different seasons of faith.

The last spiritual awakening took place during the 1960's and 1970's and was then followed by a season of *experiencing faith* and is related to those churches that are considered non-mainline churches (fundamental & charismatic). This was an exciting time for the Church of the Lord Jesus Christ as people from all walks of life were introduced to the Savior and were swept into the Kingdom.

However, since the mid 1990's we have entered into the second season of *doing faith* that once was only associated with the main-line churches but is now allied with the seeker friendly churches and those associated with the Social Justice movement. In each of these seasons, the churches associated with each have experienced growth and correspondingly, the other group has experienced a decline.

Since we have ended the season of *experiencing faith* and have entered into the season of *doing faith,* it suggests that we are headed for a secular crisis. We are now drawing closer and closer to this crisis every day and are even now experiencing its beginning.

What does that mean for the Church in general? The change that is coming certainly is not comfortable even though it is predictable. Before we address the coming change, it is healthy for us to look back and see what good and bad has occurred during the last era.

As we passed through the last spiritual awakening, we witnessed the rise of The Word of faith movement that brought back to the Church the knowledge of God's love for His people that reveal itself in supernatural ways. Millions of accounts of God's miracles of healing and deliverance have been reported throughout the whole earth. Independent/Non-denominational churches sprang up all over the world declaring the glory of God.

In the mid 1990's we began to see the other side of the coin, the emergence of the New Age movement, the anti-establishment culture, an over abundant concern for self, and a fragmentation of society where the smaller interest groups were emphasized at the expense of the national collective life. People wanted to feel good about themselves. Even in the church, we saw this happening as churches advanced the small group and cell group concept where there was less teaching and more facilitating.

Throughout the world a new awakening is emerging that has taken the Church by surprise. While the Church became concerned with itself, a counterfeit gospel of the Kingdom has flooded the world and has captured the hearts of millions of young people. Some of the largest churches in America have accepted this gospel and even the White House had a new spiritual advisor that is the spokesperson for this false gospel. The Church must keep its eyes open to fraud and deceit.

In the Church, as in society, it has become nearly impossible to build a sense of *community* and agree on anything of real substance. In our society, we see the lines being drawn in the sand for just about every area of moral concern. As each side takes their positions and as each feels the strain, one wonders how soon before we will experience a national and spiritual disaster of great consequence.

What is it that now is shaping our world and therefore will shape our future? What is it that will lead up to the Big Crisis we are all dreading? We are fast becoming a global village and with it a loss of national culture. Nationalism is no longer a viable force in our global economy. Although there are a few holdouts like North Korea and Iran, the majority of the world's governments are being drawn together into bigger alliances; i.e. the United Nations. There may be a recurrence of a few border conflicts, however, the world as a whole will bring political and financial pressure and possible military force to stop the violence for the "good" of the whole.

The Church is already affected to a BIG degree. It is no longer business as usual as in the past twenty years. When there is a shift in seasons as from the "experiencing faith" to the "doing faith", there is also see a shift in values and emphasis. Whereas people were looking for spiritual experiences in the *experiencing faith* season, we see people looking now for institutions of worship that offers an expression of *doing faith* through social justice.

What is it that we can expect to see in the coming days ahead? It may be that there will be less concern with the development of one's spiritual growth. It will be a time when people will want to do faith or be involved with social or government run programs. It will be a time of embracing the familiar and be less associated with experimentation. In other words, there will be less emphasis on developing a relationship with God through the Holy Spirit and more on religion.

There will be a religious spirit that rears its ugly head within the Church. There will be a form of Godliness but the people will deny the power of the Holy Spirit. This religious spirit will stand in the way of God's work. This religious spirit will cause the church leaders to talk but never say, "Thus says the Lord". It will tell the voice of the righteous to SHUT UP. It will cause the people to be lukewarm, judgmental, legalistic and critical.

It will be a time for the Great Society to rear its head. We may finally begin to see, that which we feared: the government taking over more and more control of our lives. We have already witnessed the struggle for the church to bar same sex marriages. We will see more and more of the values that we (the Church) hold dear begin to be washed away in the tide of floodwaters that are fast approaching our shores.

What is our Hope?

I believe that our only hope in bringing back righteousness to the earth depends on the Church preaching the Gospel of the Kingdom of God. This preaching must then be confirmed by the demonstration of power. There must also be a determined effort on the part of Church leaders to teach and promote the culture of the Kingdom.

The Church must not look to the past for answers but turn to the King. He has sent His Spirit into the world that He might lead and guide us. We must wait on Him and not panic but realize that the Kingdom is within us. We can go forth and bring God's Kingdom into this world along with the accompanying freedom and peace that only Jesus can give. The people of the world will be drawn to us as we are transformed into His image and empowered by His Spirit. They are looking for a kingdom that presents a culture that will satisfy the longing of their soul.

Here is our problem! Too many of the disciples of Jesus Christ are waiting for the next Moses, Joshua, David, or Paul to step forward and declare, "Here is the vision that God has shared with me, come and join me". However, what is needed is a clear vision of the Kingdom by Church leaders who will then proclaim it loud and clear to body of Christ.

The Church over the last forty years has seen its acceptance increase in western culture and has grown in numbers. Because of that, pastors are reluctant to make way for change, even when that change is God directed. The material and psychological benefits that come as the Church increases in size and wealth are hard for some to give up, no matter how awesome the vision. It will take a change in our worldview to move us from our present position.

The cost of pursuing a God-given Vision is more than just surrendering to change. It demands that we give it our all, even at great sacrifice. A God-given vision is always beyond our reach. Its fulfillment can never be realized by human efforts alone; God must be involved. Moreover, when God is involved that means He is to get all the glory. Dying to self and allowing the Holy Spirit to give us a humble and meek spirit must become a priority. Our dependence must be on God's ability alone no matter how intelligent, capable or learned we are.

Accepting a God given vision is not the same as receiving a dream. Dreams given by God are sometimes foretelling of future events and at other times, they are directions to be followed. In either case, they are more or less a one-time event. A God given Vision on the other hand requires hard work, perseverance and stepping out of our comfort zone.

It sometimes means going it alone until you find others that will buy into your vision. A vision that is not mainstream and runs counter to what is generally accepted will face an uphill battle to be embraced. A God given vision pushes people into the unknown and forces them to take great risks. Those that embrace such a vision can expect to be treated the same as the Apostle Paul.

Paul, Peter, Stephen and all the other Apostles and early disciples received Jesus' vision. He said, *"Go into all the world and preach the Gospel"*. They faced opposition from their fellow Jews and from the Roman government as well. Thousands of regular every day people were crucified because they would not stop until the Vision was complete. The completion of the Vision was more important than their very lives. Listen to the Voice of Martyrs and you will hear stories of people around the world that have received this same Vision and they too are putting their lives on the line for its completion.

Where do we stand with the proclamation of the, "Gospel of the Kingdom of God"? Are we holding on to the Gospel of Jesus? The good news: that Jesus came to earth to save sinners. All you need to do is just accept him as your savior and you will be saved. When you die, you will go to heaven and live with Jesus forever.

If you accept the above, you'll not be ridiculed, be laughed at or looked upon as a heretic. However, if you catch the vision of what Jesus said and the promise of God's Grand Plan, then watch out. You will be persecuted but you will find the comfort of the Holy Spirit, you will find the strength to go on, you will find an adventure of a lifetime as you walk side by side with the King. You will be empowered by the Holy Spirit and signs and wonders will follow your spreading the Gospel of the Kingdom.

The Gospel that MUST be Preached

Is the Gospel to be preached only of salvation and a ticket to Heaven when we die? Is it just the absence of tears, pain, sin, peace, sorrow, worship, etc. that we are expecting when we are face to face with Jesus? When we get to the place on the "other side", are we just going to be singing and bowing down for an eternity; or is there more to the Gospel?

Is it possible, that the Church has preached this message at the exclusion of the message that Jesus preached? Jesus Himself said that unless you are "born again" you cannot see nor can you enter the kingdom of God. Throughout the Gospels, we read that JESUS WENT ABOUT PREACHING THE GOSPEL OF THE KINGDOM.

Does the Kingdom message include, you must be "born again"? Does it include deliverance, healing, peace, freedom and more? Yes, it does; it has to because this is what Jesus preached and demonstrated. Jesus is the door into the kingdom and there is no other way we can enter the kingdom except through faith in Him.

But the message of the CROSS-IS followed by the message of the RESURRECTION. The message of the resurrection is followed by the message of Christ's ASCENSION. If we just hang out near the cross and the empty tomb, we lose understanding of the complete purpose of Christ and the Father's Grand Plan for His creation. We must understand Christ's journey included His all-important Ascension to the right hand of the Father.

Beyond the Cross and the Resurrection

If we are to fully comprehend God's Plan for us, we must understand the great importance of Christ's own personal journey. We have limited our sight of him as the pre-incarnate Christ, The incarnate Christ, the sinless Jesus, the suffering servant, the savor crucified, and the resurrected savior.

It is at the empty tomb that the church sees His mission as accomplished. We quote Jesus' own words; when He said, *"It is finished"*. Jesus declared that His work on the earth was finished. His statement confirmed that there was nothing more that could be done to accomplish our redemption (Note: Heb. 9:11-12). Therefore, we end the story there at the empty tomb.

Regarding our redemption, the above is true. His work was finished. However, that was not His purpose. It was His mission, yes, but not His purpose. What He accomplished there on the cross was just an introduction to the fulfillment of the many prophesies throughout the old testament concerning His ASCENSION to the throne.

The church has been so concerned with what God has done for man, in man and through man because of His Redeeming Grace that she has ignored the doctrine of the Ascension. Through His Ascension, God places Jesus upon a throne and declared Him to be Lord and Christ. With His exaltation, Jesus is prepared to honor His Church as she gives herself to extend His kingdom here on earth.

The great doctrine in the Gospels and Epistles that the Church is overlooking is; Christ is seated in the heavenlies, exalted at God's right hand ready to be King over His Church. His kingdom is Now.

In order for the church to be the Church, it must hear what the Spirit is saying to the Church. The Holy Spirit is revealing that Jesus the Savior is Jesus the King. His kingdom is now and the Church is to take its active role in extending His kingdom. The making of disciples is more than getting people to act like Jesus, it is equipping them to do the work of the ministry.

When we are "Born Again", we are not only placed into the family of God, we become citizens of another kingdom with all the rights and privileges of this kingdom. It is important that we get this right because this is the reason Jesus left heaven and took on the form of man. He endured the cross and accepted the shame for the joy that would follow. What is then the JOY to follow? It is our being restored into fellowship with the Father and then being placed into a position enabling us to rule with Him.

Jesus was always talking to his disciples about entering, seeing, and inheriting the Kingdom prepared for God's children. He gave us something to live for Now as well as after death. Jesus gave us this prayer... *"Thy kingdom come, thy will be done, on earth as it is in heaven."* We are to **invade** this world with the Gospel of the Kingdom and replace the world's culture with the culture of the Kingdom of God. We are to **occupy** until He comes. We are to **influence** this world, utterly, totally, completely. We are to replace the lawless world system we are living in with a kingdom of Righteousness.

So what is the Gospel of the Kingdom of God? Simply put, the Good News is that 'The King has come'! The fulfillment of the Promise has come. Jesus, the king, has come to reclaim and re-establish His Father's Kingdom here on earth. His kingdom is here and everyone is invited to enter and become a citizen.

Jesus is determined to build a Church, a body of believers that would return His Father's Kingdom on the earth to its original state. To accomplish that goal God would have many sons and daughters working with him to turn the world right side up. To accomplish this, however, requires the complete revelation of Christ. First, there is the revelation of Christ as He comes to seek and to save those that are lost. Then we have the revelation of His joining forces with His Church to extend His kingdom as they do battle against the forces of darkness.

Jesus is the only door that leads into the kingdom. Without acknowledging this we cannot be "born again" nor enter the Kingdom. It is an indispensible step but it is not the entire journey. If we focus on this first step, we will never enjoy the many blessings that belong to God's children as we mature into Sonship and are made ready to reign with Jesus. God the Father is preparing us for something BIG-something more. He expects us to extend His Kingdom here on earth. Everything God created has a purpose and only as it fulfills that purpose is GLORY revealed.

---

[i] Strauss and Howe, *Generations*

Chapter Thirteen

Our Journey – Getting close to God

Getting on the Right Path

Every one of us lives, moves and plans within a certain framework of reference (a set of ideas from which we interpreted or assigned meaning to other ideas). We have considered the Topic of *Worldviews* in Chapters 3 and 4. Our worldview, in effect will become our frame of reference. We must appreciate the fact that each person has a view of the world, of life, and of eternity that is entirely their own; made up of their life experiences, including the learning that they have had. We can safely say the higher they have climbed the learning ladder, in experience and in education, the broader their perspective.

It should be of no surprise then when Jesus encourages us to come up higher, not only to learn from Him but also to see what He sees. This is important because:

- For some, their primary interest is being saved and going to heaven. This allows them to live as they like, even if it is within certain limits.

- For some, their primary interest is the establishment of God's Law and therefore become very legalistic in their approach to life.

- Others look to their new found faith in God as a way to a better life. They see their Faith as the way to prosperity, health and all other benefits that are part of their new way of life.

- Then there are those that live only to please the Father. This is where we come to our frame of reference – It is here we begin with the Father's heart even before the foundation of the world. It begins with the eternal Father and ends with a vast family of which we are a part.

"Therefore, my beloved brethren, be steadfast, immovable, always abounding in the work of the Lord, knowing that your labor is not in vain in the Lord". 1 Cor 15:58

This statement by Paul sums up his life. He is not ashamed of the Gospel and this is the work that he dedicated his life to. *When* we come to understand what God's Grand Plan really is, *then,* like Paul, this truth will set us free from doing anything less in importance.

Purpose and Grace

God has called us to His own purpose. Just because Adam sinned and God had to extend His mercy and grace does not mean that God forgot about or overlooked His original purpose. Our journey, to reach our destination and fulfill our purpose, is necessary in order for God to workout our perfection. It is not just a journey but a time of getting intimate with God and being prepared to fulfill His Grand Plan that He has for each of us.

Here is the problem: Most Christians are not concerned with, nor do they even know about God's purpose. They have concerned themselves only with God's grace. Because they see what God has done only as it relates to and benefits them; they do not even consider the disappointment in the Father's heart when Man lost his ability to fulfill his purpose.

Consider the following diagram as you reflect on God's original purpose. From D to Z there are steps that most Christians do not think about as they live their life out here on earth.

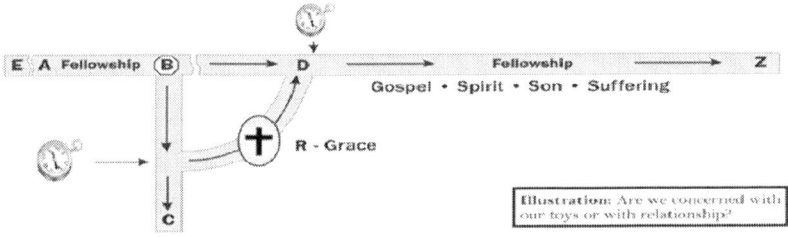

E –Eternity Past - The Correct Starting Point is The Father's Heart. All understanding of Man begins from the outpouring of the heart of the Creator, the heart of God the Father.

A – Creation – God made Man in His image and after His likeness. All things are created in order that man might fulfill God's Grand Plan.

B – Rebellion – When man is deceived, rebellion against his Creator is formed in his heart. This rebellion results in broken fellowship between man and his Creator. God is forced to send (drive) man out of His presence.

C – Captivity – Man, when left to his own devices, sinks further and further into captivity. His only hope is the mercy of God that reveals itself in a message of deliverance. The message when received, believed and acted upon is what brings his deliverance.

R – Redemption is the time of God's grace. By His grace, God makes it possible for mankind to be reconciled unto Him. God the Father restores us to a "child" relationship when we respond to His mercy by godly sorrow and a change in our heart from rebellion to obedience.

D – Justification - Our new position before God. We stand before God, with no condemnation and are able to move forward in fellowship and purpose with Him.

Z – The realization of God's Grand Plan for mankind - God's Grand Plan is for His children to mature and be transformed into the image and likeness of His Son, Jesus and then to rule and reign in righteousness with Him in His Kingdom.

The compass represents a "defining moment" when we make a decision that will affect us the rest of our lives. Note: The distance from B to C is best realized by viewing it as levels of Depravity. Some see their sin and need for reconciliation at an early level. Others travel down the road of depravity, becoming the outcasts of society, before coming to repentance and faith in Christ (Nicky Cruz of "*The Cross and the Switchblade*").

There are other "defining moments" that allow us to go deeper into the love of God. However, we must realize that each one is not the goal or the end in itself. *Conviction* of sin is not our desired result nor is the *Forgiveness* that follows. We might think that the *Reconciliation*, which comes next, is what God desires for us, but it is not. It is not even the *Relationship* that evolves. What God wants is for us to enter into an intense, intimate *Fellowship* with Him.

Is our goal D or is the goal Z? If our goal is D then we will rally around the cross and never move on toward the Grand Plan that God has for us.

However, if our goal is Z we must be involved in two tasks. First, we must take our renewed relationship (redemption) through four levels of Fellowship. Second, we must grasp and take hold of our understanding regarding our reinstated position (justification). We will say more on this subject in Chapter fifteen.

God's desire is for us to participate in 'fellowship'. Our English word, 'fellowship' is the translation of the Greek word, "*koinonia.*" In New Testament times this word was used to describe a joint-partnership in a business venture in which all parties actively participate to ensure the success of the business.[i]

In addition to being translated as fellowship it is also translated by the words, "contribution," "sharing," and "participation." A close study of the usage of this word shows that action is always included in its meaning. Fellowship is not just being together, it is doing together! It is our partnership with Christ in fulfilling God's will.

Fellowship is an inner unity expressed outwardly in action. It is not just doing anything together but it is working together to accomplish God's will.

If we are going to continue on this journey, we must not only understand why this word was used but also understand the levels of and the depth of this 'Fellowship' that God calls us.[ii]

The journey continues as we participate in the (a) Fellowship of His Gospel. We move along as we engage in the (b) Fellowship of His Spirit. As we offer ourselves as a living sacrifice, we are growing in the (c) Fellowship of His Son. The real test of our love is when we enter into the (d) Fellowship of His Sufferings.

God's has a Purpose for Man. To understand the importance of this call into fellowship we must understand God's purpose for Man. The Bible testifies to God's thoughts regarding this:

- *"Let us make man in our image and after our likeness and let them have dominion"* (Gen. 1:26-28)

- *"Be ye therefore perfect, even as your father in heaven is perfect"* (Matt. 5:48)

- *"This also we wish, even your perfection"* (2 Cor. 13:9)

- *"I travail in birth until Christ be formed in you"* (Gal. 4:9)

- *"Until we all come...unto a perfect man* (Eph. 4:13)

- *"That the man of God be perfect"* (2 Tim. 3:17)

- *"Hath called us unto glory and virtue"* (2 Pet. 1:3)

This purpose has never changed. Jesus is the first born of many sons. Hebrews 2:10 says, *"For it was fitting for Him, for whom are all things and by whom are all things, in bringing many sons to glory, to make the captain of their salvation perfect through sufferings."*

In addition, in Hebrews 1:8-9, *"But to the Son He says: "Your throne, O God, is forever and ever; a scepter of righteousness is the scepter of your kingdom. You have loved righteousness and hated lawlessness; Therefore God, Your God, has anointed You with the oil of gladness more than your companions."*

128

Levels of Fellowship

(a) Fellowship in the Gospel - Philippians 1:3-6

I thank my God upon every remembrance of you, always in every prayer of mine making request for you all with joy, for your fellowship in the gospel from the first day until now, being confident of this very thing, that He who has begun a good work in you will complete it until the day of Jesus Christ;

All Christians enjoy this common experience. It can be a very shallow experience or one of some substance. The more we have knowledge of His will, stand in agreement with His plan, grow in our affection toward Him, enjoy His presence, conform to His image, and participate in His joy the more we deepen our Fellowship of the Gospel. This is a result of spending time reading and mediating on the Word and through prayer.

When you join with others in this Fellowship of the Gospel, you are in effect joining a TEAM and become a member of its culture. When you join or fellowship at a particular church; you are joining their team. Even if there are only two of you, you are a team. The Apostle Paul continually admonished the Church to have the same mind; showing the world, that those that embrace the gospel can work in unity, they can love the unlovable, and they can forgive as they are forgiven.

Disciples are not just followers; they are messengers of the gospel. We are called out from the world to be Ambassadors of the Kingdom. The early disciples knew they were reconciled to Christ and that God was making his appeal to the world through them. There was a love that was placed within them that took a hold of their heart; they were convinced that Jesus died for all, was raised from the dead that they might no longer live for themselves but for Him.

Jesus' plan was simple. He brought together a team of twelve men who were dedicated to Him and His message. For three years He lived with, cared for, taught, corrected, trusted, forgave, and loved them. He prepared them for service and He expected them to go forth and do the same for others as He had done for them.

We are now 21st Century Disciples of Christ therefore; we hold dear, not just the teachings of Jesus, but also the person of Jesus himself. The Gospel of the Kingdom is revolutionary. It changes the heart. The Gospel, powered by His Spirit, is a gospel of love that transforms every one of us from the inside out.

No other gospel offers such promise and hope to humanity. It offers to bring man out darkness into the light. It offers peace to the troubled. It offers freedom to those that are bound. It offers forgiveness of sin, mercy, grace, health, prosperity and righteousness. It offers a future with life everlasting instead of torment and pain. When the truth of this gospel consumes us, as it did Jesus and the early Church, we will turn our world upside down.

When you are on a team, you need to have the same purpose, the same vision, the same attitude and the same level of faith or at least open to grow in your faith. You need to come under the same governmental authority or you will be divided. When you are on a team, everyone participates and the greater opportunity for success.

The question is: Is the team you're on even in the game? Is the church you are attending even out there sharing the Gospel of the Kingdom of God?

(b) Fellowship of the Spirit - Philippians 2:1-3

"Therefore if there is any consolation in Christ, if any comfort of love, if any fellowship of the Spirit, if any affection and mercy, fulfill my joy by being like-minded, having the same love, being of one accord, of one mind."

God calls us to be led by the Spirit of God in order that we can live a righteous life without condemnation. We are to walk after the Spirit and not after the flesh. This relationship with the Holy Spirit is an intense and personal relationship. When we are involved in sin, the Holy Spirit is grieved and He will quickly depart. He is unable to move in our lives when we do not allow him access to our spirit. He comes to empower us, yet He will back off when we decide to do our own thing, ignore him, or do it our own way.

To walk in fellowship of the Spirit requires a willingness to go in the same direction as the Holy Spirit. It means that we must walk together with the same conviction of purpose, hand in hand and shoulder to shoulder.

God the Father gave Jesus the responsibility to re-claim the Kingdom; this He did by the power of the Holy Spirit. Now it is time for His disciples to extend the Kingdom by the same power of the Holy Spirit. Just as Jesus relied on the Holy Spirit to accomplish His task, we must do the same to accomplish ours.

The power of the Holy Spirit is not separate from the person of the Holy Spirit. Without his presence, there is no power. Without fellowship with the Holy Spirit, our work for the Lord is our work and not His. The early disciples recognized this and joined themselves together, prayed together, worshiped together and experienced together the infilling of the Holy Spirit. They held all things in common and the Holy Spirit was pleased. He manifested His presence and the gifts of the Spirit were available to carry on the Work assigned.

Jesus said, *"I still have many things to say to you, but you cannot bear them now. However, when He, the Spirit of truth, has come, He will guide you into all truth; for He will not speak on His own authority, but whatever He hears He will speak; and He will tell you things to come. He will glorify Me, for He will take of what is Mine and declare it to you. All things that the Father has are Mine. Therefore, I said that He will take of Mine and declare it to you."* (John 16:12-15).

We continue to emphasis, that we must develop our relationship with the Holy Spirit. If we only talk about Jesus and only mention the Father when we pray, we will soon become legalistic. Furthermore, we will begin to "reason out" Scripture instead of receiving revelation from the one who has been given the responsibility to be the administrator of the Church.

Since the Holy Spirit is a spirit, it is only through our spirit that we can sense his presence. We, therefore, must develop our sensitivity to the Holy Spirit.

(c) Fellowship of the Son - 1 Corinthians 1:4-9

"I thank my God always concerning you for the grace of God which was given to you by Christ Jesus, that you were enriched in everything by Him in all utterance and all knowledge, even as the testimony of Christ was confirmed in you, so that you come short in no gift, eagerly waiting for the revelation of our Lord Jesus Christ, who will also confirm you to the end, that you may be blameless in the day of our Lord Jesus Christ. God is faithful, by whom you were called into the fellowship of His Son, Jesus Christ our Lord."

As the Holy Spirit lives to make Christ more real, we realize that we are called to go still further and deeper into Fellowship. We are exhorted to offer our total self as a living sacrifice, to have the mind of Christ, to abide in Christ, to listen to and to obey Christ. We are called to an intimacy closer than that of a husband and wife. There are no secrets, there is no doubt, there is no fear, and there is no holding back of love and sacrifice for the other. There is nothing not shared.

To have fellowship with the Son, we must align our life to having the same purpose in life as Him. We must walk in the light as He is in the light and be willing to take up our cross (the assignment that God has given to us). This fellowship with the Son involves more than our heart, it involves our feet, hands and mouth. It involves our "doing". There is no fellowship with the Son without our participating in the same work of extending His Kingdom.

More about our Fellowship with the Son follows in Chapter fourteen when we discuss "The Son of Man" and the "Internal Cross".

(d) Fellowship of His sufferings – Philippians 3:7-11

"But what things were gain to me, these I have counted loss for Christ. Yet indeed I also count all things loss for the excellence of the knowledge of Christ Jesus my Lord, for whom I have suffered the loss of all things, and count them as rubbish, that I may gain Christ and be found in Him, not having my own righteousness, which is from the law, but that which is through faith in Christ, the righteousness which is from God by faith; that I may know Him and the power of His resurrection, and the fellowship of His sufferings, being conformed to His death, if, by any means, I may attain to the resurrection from the dead."

As we present ourselves to grow in greater fellowship with our Lord, we find that it is no longer us that live, but Christ who lives in us. We find that we now consider ourselves crucified with Christ, dead to sin and alive unto God. We identify with His purposes not ours.

It is as we respond to this call to Fellowship in His Sufferings that we are prepared to enter into fruitful ministry. We must maintain our focus on His Purpose and embrace God's Grand Plan, or we will not continue on this pathway to the throne – we will take the road less traveled. See 2 Cor. 11:23-30; Phil 1:20; 2 Cor. 4: 7-11; 2 Cor. 1:1-7.

If we look around the Church today, it soon becomes obvious that men occupy themselves with only various parts of truth. It also becomes evident, that the depths of the truths we accept and our willingness to stand against the opposing arguments will reveal the "level of our fellowship."

There is no book that has stirred my heart in recent years than, *Tortured for Christ* by Richard Wurmbrand, founder of The Voice of the Martyrs. From the writings in this small volume, I began to see the true meaning of the Fellowship of His Sufferings. Suffering for righteousness sake involves more than the brutality of physical or mental cruelty.

The ungodly lash out to those that bring light into darkness. They do not want their evil deeds to be exposed. They want to protect their self-righteous image and their place in society; whether that society is family, work or community. They want to quiet the voices of those that speak up for righteousness, just as the Jewish people killed the prophets in the Old Testament. They will use ridicule, belittlement and lies to discredit the messenger of the very message that can bring them the freedom and peace that they seek.

The ungodly will use fear to persuade the righteous to back off from their rigid stand against them. They threaten to steal, kill, not only the body, but all our dreams and visions, and destroy or eradicate any sense of purpose that keeps us moving forward. They wish to crush our spirit.

Listen to Paul's comments to the Church at Corinth after his ordeals; 2 Corinthians 4. *"But we have this treasure in earthen vessels, that the excellence of the power may be of God and not of us. We are hard-pressed on every side, yet not crushed; we are perplexed, but not in despair; persecuted, but not forsaken; struck down, but not destroyed — always carrying about in the body the dying of the Lord Jesus, that the life of Jesus also may be manifested in our body. For we who live are always delivered to death for Jesus' sake, that the life of Jesus also may be manifested in our mortal flesh."*

Satan hates God's servants. When we attack his kingdom, he takes notice and assigns higher-level powers to go on the defensive. He may use family members, friends, fellow church members and even your community to stop your attack.

The question: How long will you and I continue in this fellowship of suffering as we travel toward the throne? When we have deeply entered into this fellowship with our God we find that we are participating fully with Him in His Grand Plan.

Jesus said, *"If you love me keep my commandments".* He also said, *"Do not think that I have come to destroy the law or the Prophets, I did not come to destroy but to fulfill".*

If we are going to have 'fellowship' of any depth with our God, we must know and keep the Ten Commandments. Obedience is the foundation of relationship with a King.

There are blessings and benefits that follow when we keep the Commandments:

Peace, Power to resist sin, Joy, Understanding, Strength, Freedom, Hope, Comfort in suffering, No shame, Reverence for God, A thankful heart, A worshipful heart, A clean life and Personal revival.

The Ten Commandments

I. Thou shall have no other gods beside me.

II. Thou shall not make to thyself an idol, nor likeness of anything, whatever things are in the heaven above, and whatever are in the earth beneath, and whatever are in the waters under the earth. Thou shall not bow down to them, nor serve them; for I am the Lord thy God, a jealous God, recompensing the sins of the fathers upon the children, to the third and fourth generation to them that hate me, and bestowing mercy on them that love me to thousands of them, and on them that keep my commandments.

III. Thou shall not take the name of the Lord thy God in vain; for the Lord thy God will not acquit him that takes his name in vain.

IV. Remember the Sabbath day to keep it holy. Six days thou shall labor, and shall perform all thy work. But on the seventh day is the Sabbath of the Lord thy God; on it thou shall do no work, thou, nor thy son, nor thy daughter, thy servant nor thy maidservant, your ox nor your donkey nor any cattle of your, nor the stranger that sojourns with thee. For in six days the Lord made the heaven and the earth, and the sea and all things in them, and rested on the seventh day; therefore, the Lord blessed the seventh day, and hallowed it.

V. Honor thy father and thy mother, that it may be well with thee, and that thou may live long on the good land, which the Lord thy God gives to thee.

VI. Thou shall not commit adultery.

VII. Thou shall not steal.

VIII. Thou shall not kill.

IX. Thou shall not bear false witness against thy neighbor.

X. Thou shall not covet thy neighbor's wife; thou shall not covet thy neighbor's house; nor his field, nor his servant, nor his maid, nor his ox, nor his donkey, nor any of his cattle, nor whatever belongs to thy neighbors.

---

[i] NKJV-Annotations, Philippians 1:5 page 1997
[ii] DeVern F. Fromke, *The Ultimate Intention*

Chapter Fourteen

Servant and King

The Son of Man

The Bible uses the term Son of Man 82 times in the New Testament. All, but two, are from the lips of Jesus himself. We have to wonder, why did Jesus make known this self-chosen title for Himself?

The biggest obstacle that Jesus faced was that of identity. He needed to communicate to the people of the day exactly who He was. He was not just a teacher, prophet or a priest. He was a king and not just any king but the promised messiah-the King of Glory. He needed a title that would identify himself and his mission. He needed a title that the people could recognize but the title itself could be used in such a way that it would shock them into listening.

The title comes from Daniel 7:13-14. *"I was watching in the night visions, And behold, one like the Son of Man, Coming with the clouds of heaven! He came to the Ancient of Days, and they brought Him near before Him. Then to Him was given dominion, glory, and a kingdom that all peoples, nations, and languages should serve Him. His dominion is an everlasting dominion, which shall not pass away,"*

Daniel had a vision of four empires that were so cruel that they were called beasts. However, Daniel, in his vision, was revealing that the time of their power had ended and that a new empire was coming. In Dan 7:18, he writes, *"But the saints of the Most High shall receive the kingdom, and possess the kingdom forever, even forever and ever."* The King that was to come was "The Messiah".

Because of this vision, the Nation of Israel had the expectation, that when they hear that the Son of Man has come they could expect the return of their glorious empire as under King David. This new victorious King would be the long awaited Messiah.

In Mark 2:5-12 we read of the story of the paralyzed man lowered through the roof so that Jesus could heal him. *"When Jesus saw their faith, He said to the paralytic, 'Son, your sins are forgiven you. 'And some of the scribes were sitting there and reasoning in their hearts, 'Why does this Man speak blasphemies like this? Who can forgive sins but God alone?'"*

But immediately, when Jesus perceived in His spirit that they reasoned thus within themselves, He said to them, "Why do you reason about these things in your hearts? Which is easier, to say to the paralytic, 'Your sins are forgiven you,' or to say, 'Arise, take up your bed and walk'?

But that you may know that the **SON OF MAN** *has power on earth to forgive sins"* — *He said to the paralytic, "I say to you, arise, take up your bed, and go to your house." Immediately he arose, took up the bed, and went out in the presence of them all, so that all were amazed and glorified God, saying, "We never saw anything like this!"*

Jesus proclaimed that He was God but said more by what He called Himself, The Son of Man. Jesus, by identifying himself as the Son of Man, was proclaiming to be the Messiah and therefore, ushering in the Kingdom that would have dominion forever and forever.

However, the Nation of Israel, having been subjected to humiliation and dishonor, was not looking for a gentle and humane Messiah. They could not imagine a Messiah, such as the man named Jesus, who could lead them to greatness and power.

How they got to this point is possibly based on the Inter-testament book of Enoch. In this book, the Son of Man is always a divine figure waiting in the heavenly places to be unleashed in vengeance and in judgment upon the world. He reigns in triumph and then shares that triumph with the faithful.

Also in Psalm 2:7, a psalm long regarded as a Messianic Psalm, it speaks of the Son begotten of God and pictures His triumph and the judgment executed upon His enemies. *"I will declare the decree: the Lord hath said unto me, Thou art my Son; this day have I begotten thee. Ask of me, and I shall give thee the heathen for thine inheritance, and the uttermost parts of the earth for thy possession. Thou shalt break them with a rod of iron; thou shalt dash them in pieces like a potter's vessel"*

The following two Scriptures, however, reveal yet another picture of the Messiah. They bring together the idea of the suffering servant and the triumphant Messiah in Jesus.

In Isaiah 42:1, the writer begins to draw his picture of God's servant but does not complete it until he puts the finishing strokes to the canvas in Isaiah 53.

When Jesus speaks of himself as the Son of Man, we see him as someone who has nowhere to lay his head, is persecuted and as one who has come to seek and save the lost. He identifies himself as one coming, not to be served but to serve and to give his life as a ransom for many; not coming to destroy men's lives but to save them.

The disciples were at first confused and not ready to accept this new picture of their Messiah. Even though Jesus spoke often of his death and the resurrection, they still could not see the complete picture because of what was already painted in their mind; that of a conquering king who would destroy their enemies and pronounce judgment upon them.

The reason for the above goes back to what we discussed regarding the Jellybeans. The human mind will shut off anything that it does not expect to see, accept or understand. The disciples connected the Son of Man with majesty, power and glory, not with the idea of suffering, humiliation and death.

It was the resurrection that made the difference in the thinking of the disciples. If the story ended with His suffering and death, it would have been impossible for the early Church to see Jesus as the fulfillment of the Son of Man as depicted by Isaiah. The resurrection however, brought the suffering, the triumph, and the glory together to complete the picture.

Be of the Same Mind

If we are to delight in the fellowship of the Son, and therefore realize God's Grand Plan of reigning with Him, we must see ourselves as servants; while at the same time know that we are royalty. This is the point of seeing Jesus as the Son of Man.

This is not an easy task. We are to humble ourselves to be servants and at the same time be meek that we might exercise our position as Royalty.

God was not satisfied with just giving man a natural family and a material dwelling. God did not just create man who was then to be on his own. But in His wisdom, He brought man into His house, not as a servant but as a son.

- *For as many as are led by the Spirit of God, these are sons of God. For, you did not receive the spirit of bondage again to fear, but you received the Spirit of adoption by whom we cry out, "Abba, Father." The Spirit Himself bears witness with our spirit that we are children of God, and if children, then heirs — heirs of God and joint heirs with Christ, if indeed we suffer with Him, that we may also be glorified together.* (Rom. 8:15-17, emphasis added)

- *For it was fitting for Him, for whom are all things and by whom are all things, in bringing many sons to glory, to make the captain of their salvation perfect through sufferings. For both He who sanctifies and those who are being sanctified are all of one, for which reason He is not ashamed to call them brethren, saying: "I will declare Your name to*

> *My brethren; In the midst of the assembly I will sing praise to You."*
> (Heb 2:10-12, emphasis added)

God the Father makes all His plans with the Son in mind. His goal is that in the coming ages, Jesus might have a glorious body in which to express His very life. This body is a family of brothers and sisters whom He might have fellowship and would share His reign.

2 Tim 2:11-12

> *This is a faithful saying: For if we died with Him,*
> *We shall also live with Him. If we endure,*
> *We shall also reign with Him.*

Rev 20:6

> *Blessed and holy is he who has part in the first resurrection. Over such the second death has no power, but they shall be priests of God and of Christ, and shall reign with Him a thousand years.*

Rev 3:21

> *To him who overcomes I will grant to sit with Me on My throne, as I also overcame and sat down with My Father on His throne.*

The Internal Cross-God's Guiding Principle

In order for us to understand the Divine Principle that guides all of God's actions, we need to comprehend the relationship that exists in the Godhead, between the Father, Son and Holy Spirit. The basis of our Christian belief is that we acknowledge that there is one God existing as three eternal and co-equal Beings, the same in substance (essence) but distinct in subsistence (life).

Each has a different role to execute in this relationship. The Father is the authority while the Son fulfills the will of the Father. The Spirit speaks not of Himself but dedicates His activities to revealing the Son and fulfilling the desires of the Father and the Son.

The Father's intent is to exalt His Son who is under His authority and the Son serves that authority so that his purposes can be carried out. This is a relationship where there is no conflict and where there is perfect unity. The one in authority uses His authority benevolently for the good of those under Him and the one under Him responds with respect and with a servant's heart.

It is God's desire that we experience the same fellowship, love, peace, joy and unity of purpose that exists in the Godhead. In other words, our relationships here on earth should be such that, no one lives for themselves but for each other.

> **Point to Embrace:** What the Father, Son and Holy Spirit are revealing to the Church today is that there was not only an external cross (Calvary) **but also there is an "internal" Cross.**

The Fruit of the Spirit: love, joy, peace, longsuffering, gentleness, goodness, faith, meekness, temperance, is a result of the Holy Spirit flowing through us. It is also the result of the internal cross in us. You cannot separate the manifestation of God's presence from the person of God. You cannot separate the cross principal from God and you cannot separate the "internal cross" from the Christian. "Internal" expresses the POWER that is in the word itself.

As the gold thread in the Priest's garment is interwoven into the fabric, so the cross must be interwoven into the fabric of our lives. The gold is separate from the other threads but it is such an integrated part of the design that it cannot be removed without destroying the cloth and therefore the garment.

In order for God to reclaim His Kingdom, man must be set free from the bondage to sin and be declared justified. To accomplish this, God has revealed the external Cross of Christ that we might understand the character of His love.

The real problem for man is this: man sees the cross only as it relates to him. He does not see how it relates to God and to the realizing of His Grand Plan.[i]

Man was created to be a body for the Son that He might express Himself in the Earth and be a joint heir with Him. Salvation from Hell is not the main reason for the Son's coming to earth but a necessary reclaiming action (an action to fix a problem).

In the garden, Adam missed seeing the "Internal" Cross of the Father. It was the desire of the Father that this "Internal" Cross be in His children as it is in Him and in His only begotten Son. It was to be their manner and purpose in life, a guiding principle. You are invited to embrace the Cross Principle as a manner of life. It cannot be thrust upon you. It is not just to be chosen once – at the time of salvation - but must become the principle that guides all your actions.

If we are going to take this journey toward fulfilling God's Grand Plan, we must understand and embrace the following CENTRAL TRUTH – The Cross is an inherent part of the character of God. It is demonstrated by the Son and revealed by the Holy Spirit. This same principle must also be the guiding rule in our life.

---

[i] DeVern Fromke, *The Ultimate Intention*

Chapter Fifteen

Our New Position

A Life subject to a New Ruler

In Chapter Thirteen, we considered that our renewed relationship (redemption) takes us down the pathway through four levels of Fellowship. Now we will consider another aspect of our journey as we come to understand our reinstated position (justification).

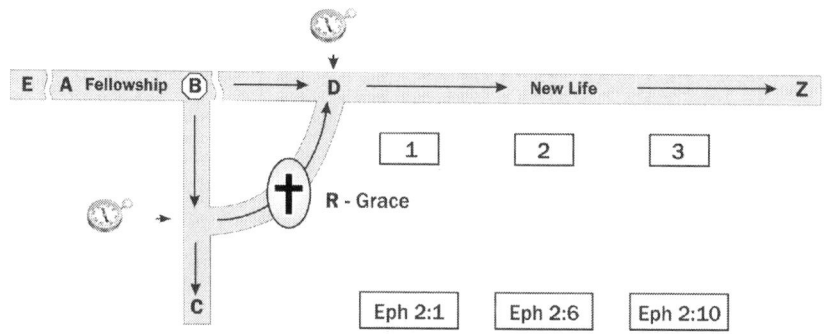

As we progress down the Pathway to the Throne, Paul emphasizes that there are three areas of New Life training that we must go through. 1. The New Life we are living has **Resurrection Power**; for we are made alive with Christ, 2. The New Life we are living has **Royal Power**; for we are seated with Christ in the heavenly places, 3. The New Life we are now living has **Reconciliation Power**; for the life of God is being manifested through us to be a blessing to others.

This power is ours to use but it is not our own, as if we have it to benefit self. It is ours to use to bring glory and honor to our king. We have been justified, making it possible for God to pour out His spirit upon us. Justification makes it possible for us to be the New Wineskins for the New Wine.

Resurrection Power

The Cross of Christ and our internal cross bring death to the "old-self" life but without Resurrection Power to raise us from death, we would not be able to live in newness of life. We would be free from the penalty of sin but not able to live with power over sin. Resurrection Power is the Power for a New Life.

In Chapter three we studied the importance of the mind. When we begin to think differently, we begin to act differently. Paul tells us to offer our total being as a sacrifice to God. He then tells us we need to think differently when he says, *"be not conformed to this world but be transformed by the renewing of your mind"*. This is a must for us because until we were "born again", we were slaves to the desires of the flesh and subject to the prince of the power of the air. These habits of the flesh now have to be overcome. We overcome by the way we think; as we think differently we act differently.

This is what we need to think about, just as the Father did not leave Jesus to suffer corruption in death, so He does not leave us to suffer without power to live a new life without righteousness. He has made us alive in Christ because it is our faith and identification with Him that allows us to walk in this newness of life.

Paul writes to the Church in Galatia, that he is no longer searching for righteousness by trying to adhere to the Law but he is in fact dead to the Law. He has had a transformation in his mind and spirit by faith; he has died with Christ and the resurrected Christ now lives in him. The life he is now living he lives by faith in the Son of God who loves him.

This Resurrection Power that we now possess, allows us to 'reckon' ourselves dead to sin and alive unto God. This word, 'reckon' is a banking term that means to know and consider what is in our account. Since we can withdraw from our account, we can live victoriously.

Sin no longer reigns in our body because we have power; a power greater than sin. Sin has no more dominion over us because we are not under the law but under grace.

The Apostle Paul writes, *"And I pray your whole spirit and soul and body be preserved blameless unto the coming of our Lord Jesus Christ."* (1 Thess. 5:23). He writes this because he knows that the Lord is coming back for a glorious Church without spot or wrinkle, a victorious Church full of power.

If we are not living in this Resurrection Power, then our travel down the pathway to the throne will be filled with disillusionment, despair, heartache and hopelessness. You will be like Lot's wife who turned around to look back at that which had been left behind and was turned into a pillar of salt or the farmer Jesus describes when He said, *"No one, having put his hand to the plow, and looking back, is fit for the kingdom of God."* (Luke 9:62).

Royal Power

Resurrection Power by itself would have been enough to shout about but God has even better things in store for His redeemed. The Father does not want to wait until His wrath is fully unleashed against the devil and then is banished to the Lake Fire before He exercises dominion over His earth.

From the beginning, He has decreed that Man would have dominion over the earth. He is not going to usurp man's authority and take control himself. He already had devised a plan that would allow man to start having dominion even before Christ returns as King of kings and Lord of lords.

The heaven where God resides is not just a place out there in the universe. The heaven that Paul is referring to is the highest place. It is the seat of God's government. It is the place of much activity. Angels are being dispatched throughout the whole earth as ministering spirit to the saints. There is a voice that sound like thunder when the Father is speaking.

It is from here that King Jesus is ruling in the lives of the Redeemed by the power of the Holy Spirit. Angels are opening the vaults of heaven as the saints are using the Keys of the Kingdom to unlock the blessings of heaven. Because of our position with Christ in the heavenlies, Believers are using His name to heal the sick, cast out demons and setting the captives FREE.

Royalty does not need to be in the place of government to exercise its rule. Because of our identity with Christ, we can rule here on Earth as his representatives and as part of the royal family. By virtue of our position (having been justified and sitting, by identification, with Christ in the Heavenlies), we have been given the RIGHT to rule and take dominion; we are citizens of the kingdom.

Christ has ALL authority and He has given to us, His royal brethren, more than the right to use this authority, He has commissioned us to go forth and continue the works of God until all nations are under His feet.

Reconciliation Power

We need Resurrection Power to live a holy life and stay connected with God. We need Royal Power to fight the onslaught of the enemy. We need Reconciliation Power to fulfill the Great Commission. This Reconciliation Power is the power of Love. We are created to do good works and there is no other way we can do unto others that brings Glory to God without Love.

Love is at the heart of the Creator; therefore, it is at the very heart of the kingdom and the culture that originates from the throne. This 'love' for others to do good works does not come naturally. It is brought about only through the work of the Holy Spirit. God's love is a self-denial, self-sacrificing expression that comes from the Man's whole person, his spirit, soul and body.

A sacrifice means nothing if it is not done willingly and completely. Just as the sacrifices in the Old Testament were killed, drained of blood and then burnt upon the alter bringing a sweet smelling aroma to the nostrils of God-so we must offer ourselves as a living sacrifice in order that Jesus might fill us with His life and love for others. Our sacrifice is the only way our good works will be looked upon as gold, silver or precious stones.

As the manna from Heaven fed the people that they might have physical life, Jesus is the Bread of Life given for us that we might partake and eat fully of the whole loaf and have Reconciliation Power and bring His life to others.

The good works that we do will show the world that God, the creator of all, loves them. Our good works will bring them to a place where the Holy Spirit can do His job of convicting of sin, righteousness and judgment.

As we embrace each of the above components of our New Life, we are progressing toward becoming an *OverComer*. As we become an OverComer, we will show power over sin and over our enemy in our life. As an OverComer, we will take authority over our enemy and take back what he has stolen. As an OverComer, we will show forth His glory in all that we do as we live unto God.

Leadership Effectiveness Training

In the late 80's and early 90's I conducted management seminars for small businesses and leadership Seminars for Pastors. In these seminars, I taught that there are three phases of growth that each must go through in order to achieve success. Growth has to occur in Character, Ability and Leadership.

Maturing: The Bible speaks of a person, having matured into adulthood, as having reached a place in their life as being responsible, trustworthy, faithful, unconditional in love, and having a positive attitude toward work and giving. It represents a life of being in oneness

144

with God. The Father has given to the Spirit the work of maturing the new child of God and bringing about full-Sonship. The Father gives as a gift –His life, His nature, His Spirit and His love. Nevertheless, growth into the very character of Jesus is the product of training, overcoming, discipline, trial, hardship, and intensive spiritual qualifying (See 2 Tim 2:15; 3:16).

The outstanding characteristic of the modern day Church goes beyond shallowness, it borders on superficiality. Our attitude toward the Bible reveals that we have not taken it seriously. We must take it as it is, and allow it to speak to us. Reading the Bible is not enough. It takes thought and meditation or we will read into Scripture the results of our own reasoning and that will be to our own destruction. Because of our lack of accurate knowledge, we will make the wrong assumptions and then draw the wrong conclusions.

To bring about maturity in the Believer, is the job of the Church and Family working with the Holy Spirit. The Church, however, has changed from having a Fathering mentality (using the five-fold ministry gifts to mentor the saints) to a church of attendees who are spectators and consumers of a "bless me" message given by a one-man show.

The Church must decide what they are going to present to their adherents based on what God has called them to do. Maturing has to do with relationships, exercising authority and doing good works. The Church must begin to mature its people in the area of citizenship and prepare them to be OverComers.

Preparing: The Apostle John tells us that Jesus increased in wisdom and in stature. Therefore, if we desire to reign with Him we also must increase in wisdom and stature.

We are destined for the throne but we must be prepared to reign. This is our inheritance. We must go through many varied experiences in order that our lives are thoroughly brought under the control of the Holy Spirit.

These experiences are like doors that we must pass through. We must surrender to the purpose of each experience. As we pass through each door, we gain wisdom. When it is our time to reign with Christ, we will use this wisdom for His glory.

We must keep our eyes on God's Grand Plan – His Purpose. If not, our experiences will not be inter-connected and they will not lead to our destination. As a train must be on the track and all the cars must be connected, so our experiences must be related and in line with the Father's purpose.

This is so very different from the present day explanation given for Romans 8:28-29, "And *we know that all things work together for good to those who love God, to those who are the called according to His purpose."* The Church today presents this verse as saying – Whatever comes our way it is God's will and we are to accept it. The church totally ignores the fact that we must be walking in accordance to His purpose. It is then and only then, things will work out for our good.

We may be "born again" but this alone does not qualify us to reign. To participate in all that preparation encompasses, comes only to those who live unto the Father's purpose. Paul admonishes us when he writes, *"Brethren, do not be children in understanding; however, in malice be babes, but in understanding be mature."* (1 Cor. 14:20).

Discussion: What then do we make of certain genuine experiences, such as salvation, separation, consecration, Baptism in the Holy Spirit, healing? Can these be just like a series of crises through which the Holy Spirit leads the hungry heart in its quest for truth or are they to prepare us for something we are to do?

Governing: Governing is more than leadership. Leadership is more than management. It is more than having the ability to control. It is all of these combined along with having purpose, being a visionary, having knowledge, understanding and exercising wisdom.

If one is going to govern, he must know where he is going, know how to get there and know what to do once he's there. He must have an 'end' in mind.

If someone is destined for Governing a nation, he/she must have knowledge of the many aspects of government. In Chapter nine, we listed nine elements of government: Constitution/laws, Taxation, Security, Justice, Commerce, Education, Citizenship, Health and Covenants. We might use these same elements for a home or a business.

God has entitled His people to have dominion over this earth (govern). To do so we must have understanding of the purpose and who is to be governed. We must have a comprehensive – see the big picture as God sees it. We must be compassionate, merciful, sympathetic, kind, good and patient.

Wisdom is an absolute necessity if one is to govern and this wisdom comes from God alone. It is not just sitting upon a throne, but executing righteousness in doing the will of the Father that speaks of our right to rule. Wisdom is using the knowledge, understanding we have obtained in order for us to make sound judgments. Wisdom allows us to make sound judgments time and time again.

Created to Rule

To satisfy His desire to share His life with another, God the Father created a visible kingdom that mirrored the invisible Kingdom of Heaven. In order to share His life, He created Man.

If God was going to create earth and establish upon it a kingdom to rule, He must either rule it himself or put someone else in charge. A king does not appoint a non-citizen or a slave to rule over his kingdom. To do so would put his kingdom at peril. A king looks for loyal, trusted, tested, honest and trustworthy men and women to put in such an important position. He confers this honor to citizens that take an "oath of allegiance".

To qualify for the throne, it requires that we have passed the test when confronted by our enemy and are willing to face the stones and arrows of this world. It requires that we have shown the righteous exercise of authority over the domain that we have been given. It requires that we have remained obedient even in the face of suffering. Paul is a perfect example of someone who experienced the beatings and then writes from that experience when he says:

- *The Spirit Himself bears witness with our spirit that we are children of God, and if children, then heirs — heirs of God and joint heirs with Christ, if indeed we suffer with Him, that we may also be glorified together.* (Rom. 8:16-18)

- *If we endure, we shall also reign with Him.* (2 Tim 2:12)

God's first call to Man was for him to have dominion over the earth and his last call to him is to reign with Him above the highest heavens. To enter into such joint position with the Lord Jesus is almost beyond our comprehension. However, to rule in righteousness is our mandate.

The writer of Hebrews states in Chapter 1, verses 8-9, AMP, "*But as to the Son, He says to Him, Your throne, O God, is forever and ever (to the ages of the ages), and the scepter of Your kingdom is a scepter of absolute righteousness - of justice and straightforwardness. You have loved righteousness - You delighted in integrity, virtue and uprightness in purpose, thought and action - and you have hated lawlessness (injustice and iniquity).*" (Emphasis added).

Our concept of governing must come from only one source, God Himself. If we do not have within us the realization that we are to one-day rule and reign with Christ, we will remain – knowing but never doing. We must be transformed to acquire a heart of a ruler. Some in the Church understand the concept of the kingdom, of having dominion and taking authority over sin, sickness and poverty, but still have never received the vision of ruling with Christ.

The Peter Principle is the principle that says, "In a hierarchy every employee tends to rise to his level of incompetence." In other words, its members are promoted so long as they work competently but then are promoted to a position they are no longer proficient and then remain there until they leave. In the Kingdom of God, to govern is not based on our ability but on our availability. The Holy Spirit empowers us to do and succeed.

Do you consider yourself a loyal citizen of the Kingdom or just a slave or a servant to Jesus? Do you consider yourself a citizen of the Kingdom of God, ready to fulfill your destiny and the hope of your calling each day?

This message of the Gospel of the Kingdom of God is the "Good News" that Jesus invites all into His Father's kingdom. In addition, upon entry He restores their citizenship rights and makes it possible for them to represent his Father's kingdom by giving to them His Spirit. This is why throughout this book we have been talking about God's Grand Plan. That plan has always been for the Father to have a family of sons like unto his only begotten Son, Jesus.

It is the Father's intent for the Son of God to have brethren in which He could express himself here on earth and for the Holy Spirit to have a temple in which to dwell and manifest the power of God. This can only be accomplished through a maturing process. It is our Father's Grand Plan that we will someday rule and reign with His only begotten Son, Jesus. The unusual aspect about all this is that all the mature citizens are sons of the Father.

Unless you know that you are a Citizen of the Kingdom of God, you will never still the storm, cast out devils, heal the sick, raise the dead, or turn water into wine.

Chapter Sixteen

A Son Placed

Adoption

There are many varied renderings of the meaning of adoption used throughout the Old Testament. Some of these are very similar to the meaning that is in use today. In the New Testament, only Paul uses this word.

"For the earnest expectation of the creation eagerly waits for the revealing of the sons of God. For the creation was subjected to futility, not willingly, but because of Him who subjected it in hope; because the creation itself also will be delivered from the bondage of corruption into the glorious liberty of the children of God.

For we know that the whole creation groans and labors with birth pangs together until now. Not only that, but we also who have the firstfruits of the Spirit, even we ourselves groan within ourselves, eagerly waiting for the adoption, the redemption of our body". Rom 8:18-24

We must understand that God does not "adopt" believers as children; they are "Born Again" into His family by the Holy Spirit, through faith. John 1:12, *"But as many as received him, to them gave he power to become the sons of God..."* KJV

Vine's Expository Dictionary of Biblical Words[i] notes that the KJV does not discriminate between the two Greek words, *teknon* and *huios* that are used throughout the New Testament to denote children and sons. There is a difference and the difference is important to note because we come into the kingdom as 'children' but through the maturing process, we grow into 'sons'.

The Gk word *teknon* is used in the above verse. The Gk. *Teknon* means to beget, to bear. It is prominent in the fact of birth and is used of children who are learners.

When the Gk word, *huios* is used throughout the New Testament, it denotes 'sons' and stresses the dignity and character of the relationship. This Gk word is used in Romans 8:19.

"Adoption" is a term involving the dignity of the relationship of believers as sons; it is not a putting into the family by spiritual birth, but a putting into the position as sons. The term as used in a theological sense commonly denotes, "a specific act of God by which He restores penitent and believing men to their privileges as members of the divine family and makes them heirs of heaven."[ii]

Romans 8:19 uses the GK word, 'Apokalupsis' meaning, "Revealing". This refers to taking the cover off, exposing something hidden from view. All creation and we ourselves are groaning within ourselves-eagerly waiting the revealing of the 'sons of God'. Surely it is as Apostle Jonas Clark has said, "Only the sons of God, led by the Spirit of God will manifest the kingdom of God".

In the parable of the prodigal son, the wayward son returns home glad to confess that he is unworthy to be called a son. He had dismissed the desire of the Father to be of little consequence and of little value. Just as Esau had sold his birthright, the prodigal son had walked away from his inheritance. The point to be observed is; by Redemption and Justification, the prodigal son was not only forgiven and reconciled to his merciful father; he was restored to the position of a son.

Adoption has the thought behind it of a "son placed". It was the practice of kings to place their sons, heirs to their throne, under the tutelage of professionals. These teachers would train them in all aspects of becoming a ruler of the kingdom. Kings gave to the tutors the responsibility of instilling into their sons, the very heart of the king. We learn from the life of Moses, that "when he was fully grown" he went out to visit his relatives. The "fully grown" suggests that when the Egyptians had completed his training, he went out to visit the Hebrews.

Today, when a man has established himself in business and has a son, his greatest hope is that his son will follow his example and take over the business. He does not take this casually. Over the years, he has put his sweat, blood and tears in the building of his business. His desire is for his son to run his business with the same dedication, the same set of values and principles that he ascribed to and will continue to build the business so that he might pass it on to his children. This training may involve working in the business as a janitor, a stock boy, salesperson, manager, etc, and most assuredly in today's economy, going to the university.

In the day of Apostle Paul, male children were placed in the hands of entrusted servants to train and teach them to act and think in such a way as to prepare them for the life they were to lead upon becoming of age. Today, we send our children off to college or to a technical school to learn a trade or profession that will enable them to earn a living.

The Jewish people have kept the tradition and the significance of the above truths alive through three major events.

Major events in a Hebrew boy's life

- *Circumcision* – Occurs at infancy when eight days old. This is a time when he is marked as a "covenant man"

- *Bar-Mitzvah* – This takes place when he was about to enter into puberty. The word Bar-Mitzvah means "a son accountable". He was now held accountable for keeping the Commandments of God and became an apprentice under his father in the family business.

- **Adoption Ceremony** – Gk *"Huiothesis"* –means "son placement" and indicates the time when a male child reached the age of maturity. The father would place his hand on his son's head and proclaim, *"This is my beloved son in whom I am well pleased. I now bestow upon him all of my riches and power and authority so that he might act on my behalf in all my affairs"*.

It is time that the Church takes seriously the orders that it has received from the Lord of the Church to prepare His bride for His return. We would think it was a dereliction of duty if a college did not prepare its students to enter the work force with the appropriate instruction or our armed forces to send troops into battle without the right training. Why then do we not think it is a dereliction of duty for the Church to send it members out unprepared to fight against it enemies, let alone unprepared to rule and reign with Christ?

It is the responsibility of the Church and the five-fold ministry to provide the training for the 'children' of God so that they may mature into the mighty warriors for Christ and some day rule and reign with Him.

Can You Imagine

Prince William, when he was born, was heir apparent to the throne of England. The whole country, even the world, recognized that he was someone special. He was Royalty. His life was destined to be different from others because he is to be different. Long before he was born, everything was put into place that would prepare him to accept his calling as King.

In order for William to be King, he needed to have certain qualities of character that would blossom forth when he took the throne. Special attention would be given to his education, manners, diet, his formed worldview, his understanding of warfare, his vision, his spiritual life, the understanding of his mission and his relationship with those he would one day rule. Consideration would be given to those whom he would choose as friends, companions and advisors. His tutors would be chosen with great care. He would receive knowledge and understanding in order to have the wisdom needed to rule and reign.

WHAT IF, however, immediately after he was born, he was whisked away to some far off country whose culture was completely different, totally opposite to that of England?

And WHAT IF, when he was 8 or 13, or 18, or 28 years old (age makes no difference) it was discovered that he was indeed the heir to the throne of England?

He would immediately be taken back to England, loved and accepted by all. However, it would be discovered, that by his character and actions, he is not prepared to mount the steps to the throne. He is a citizen by birth but that in itself does not prepare him to rule and reign. He knows nothing of his mission, has no vision, does not know of the authority that is his and has not heard the call upon his life. He knows nothing of the humility and the sacrifice required; for the honor, that is his.

AS BELEIVERS, we are very much like this stolen child. We were stolen but now are redeemed. And just as William, in the above story, needed to be changed from the inside out, we too need this transformation process to take place in our lives if we are to have Christ formed in us. We are to be changed into the very image of Christ – for that is what qualifies us for the throne.

Liberty is not a License

We have discussed previously the term 'Internal Cross' and how it is often overlooked. We concluded that, for man to have fellowship with the Father, he must have within him, the same heart of love that is characterized by the cross. We saw that the journey to the fulfillment of the Father's Grand Plan can only be realized when the Internal Cross becomes a reality in our lives.

In order to progress toward the throne, we must understand the "New Life" that must be allowed to mature within us. That new life is "His Life", the life of Christ. It is a life of righteousness and justice.

I was in Poland when it was under communist rule and witnessed firsthand the oppression they suffered. I witnessed the psychological affect it had on them. They wanted freedom but they also needed a leader who could show them how to live as a free people. When The

Berlin Wall fell in the late 1980's, I recall thinking, what are these people going to do with their newfound freedom. "They don't know how to be free."

We have read of people in Africa who were suddenly freed from their oppressors, but then just ran around stealing and doing all kinds of crazy things. They had always been told what to do, when to do it and how to do it. They did not know how to think for themselves. They thought that their newfound freedom meant License, allowing them to do whatever they wanted. They knew nothing of responsibility and accountability.

Even the 'Children' of God are very much like this. Why is this so? Children, wherever they are, view 'freedom' differently than mature adults

Unlike the above examples, Adam had known what it was to be free. God placed Adam in the Garden of Eden as a FREE moral agent. He was Free to serve whomever, his creator or self. It was his choice. He let Satan deceive him and he made the choice to serve self, which put him under the dominion of Satan.

We are born in sin and under bondage. Therefore, spiritually, like the people of Poland and Africa, we don't know what it is to be free either. When Christ sets us free from sin and death, this is a new experience for us. We don't know what to do with our newfound freedom. We too have a choice to serve a man centered religion or serving a God who so loved us that he gave Himself for us that we might have life and that more abundantly. When a slave is freed, his freedom is his to give away.

Freedom is a Transition Point

Man has misunderstood the concept of freedom. He sees his freedom as a means for self-centeredness instead of seeing it as something that is his to give away. The purpose of the finished work of Christ on Calvary is to provide for the liberation of every man. In this liberation, man is now able to choose to live under a new rule: to be a love-slave unto God or a captive under the Law.

Children need to ask, "*Well then, shall we keep on sinning so that God can keep on showing us more and more kindness and forgiveness?*

As they grow in faith and mature, they will be able to answer like the Apostle did, "*Of course not! Should we keep on sinning when we don't have to? For sin's power over us was broken when we became Christians and were baptized to become a part of Jesus Christ; through his death the power of your sinful nature was shattered. Your old sin-loving nature was buried with him by baptism when he died; and when God the Father, with glorious power, brought him back to life again, you were given his wonderful new life to enjoy."*

If we desire true freedom, we will seek first the Kingdom of God and His Righteousness. It is within the Kingdom of God that we find real liberty and when we do, we will invest our freedom by yielding to Jesus Christ.

---

[i] Copyright © 1985, Thomas Nelson Publishers

[ii] *Unger's Bible Dictionary, The New Unger's Bible Dictionary,* (Moody Press of Chicago, Illinois. Copyright © 1988

Chapter Seventeen

The Gate and The Way

A defining Moment - Living with a New Vision

Jesus said, *"Enter by the narrow gate; for wide is the gate and broad is the way that leads to destruction, and there are many who go in by it. Because narrow is the gate and difficult is the way which leads to life, and there are few who find it.* (Matt. 7:13-14).

Jesus was bringing them to a *defining moment* when they had had to decide which Way they would take: the Broad Way or the Narrow Way. He is bringing us to that same defining moment.

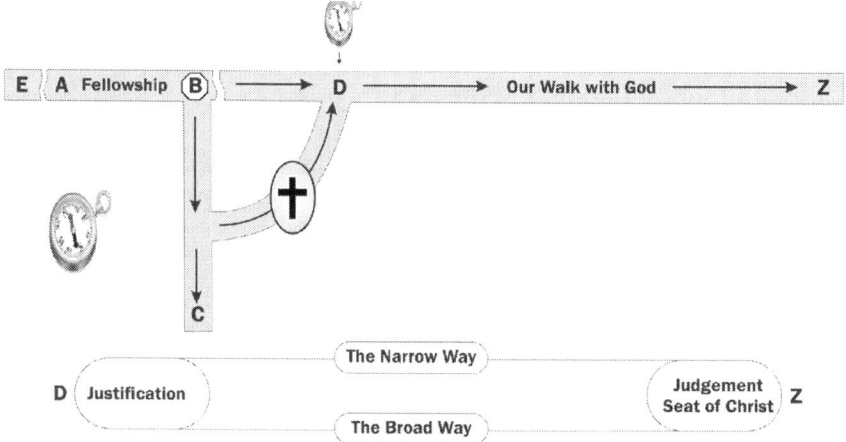

This verse is all too often applied to the unbeliever, but Jesus is here speaking to the believer. Even believers have a difficult time in making this decision to take the Narrow Way. However, we must walk in the way if we are to avoid Satan from stealing, killing or destroying the faith that the Son of God has died to bring to us.

Jesus comes to reclaim and to re-establish His Kingdom. He comes into the midst of the kingdoms of this earth and His mission is to call out a people from the world unto Himself. His desire is to paint a picture of His Father's kingdom. In this sermon, He is giving the Holy Spirit truths that He can use to penetrate the hearts of those in the sound of His voice and now through the written Word.

Before Jesus began His Sermon on the Mount, He tells the people to repent, have a change in their thinking regarding the Kingdom because it is at hand. He then preached this beautiful message; we refer to it as the Sermon on the Mount. He started with giving eight statements that we refer to as the Beatitudes.

Jesus then went on to explain the culture of the kingdom that was to be accepted and lived-out by the citizens. Jesus elaborated on what they already knew and explained the greater requirement of righteousness that exceeds the Scribes and Pharisees. Jesus turned their thinking upside down when He gave them insight into the truths about giving, praying and fasting. His teaching on the Law regarding murder, divorce, and adultery go way beyond anything they have ever heard before. The demands of the Kingdom must have caused great bewilderment, confusion and for some, disbelief.

He talked in detail about their relationship with God the Father. He described how they were to live in the world and yet, at the same time, live in the presence of the Father. Before He was through, He covered all aspects of life in the Kingdom.

One thing is perfectly clear; we cannot be citizens in both kingdoms or be a part of two cultures. Paul says it plainly to the Church in Corinth, *"Come out from among them and be separate, says the Lord. Do not touch what is unclean, and I will receive you."* *'I will be a Father to you, and you shall be My sons and daughters, says the Lord Almighty."* 2 Cor 6:17-18

In the verse quoted at the beginning of this chapter, Jesus, as a Master Teacher stops for a moment and gives His hearers time to reflect on what they have just heard. He is calling for a decision but unless they comprehend, they will not be willing to make a break with the world. They must take time to examine their attitudes in general and their disposition toward the teaching just presented.

As the margins on the page of a book give the reader time to digest what is read, time must be given between the stimulus (His words) and the response (their decision) because it will change their lives for an eternity. Will they take the narrow way that leads to abundant life or the broad way that leads to destruction? At the gate, a decision needs to be made, will they enter or not?

What Jesus was saying was, "There is no point in listening further to this sermon; if you are not going to take it to heart. What are you going to do about what you have heard?"

He offered them a choice; He now offers us a choice. Are we going to enter this revelation of the Kingdom or are we going to stay the

156

same? Has the Holy Spirit been speaking to your spirit or only to your mind?

In other words, our interest in The Kingdom of God is useless and valueless, unless we take hold of the truths within it. These truths will enable us to stand during the darkest and most critical hours of our lives.

The Kingdom Life

The Kingdom Life is a life to be entered only through a narrow gate. It is not a way of life that is, at first broad and then gets narrower. No! The gate itself is narrow. It is not entered without first having received forgiveness and being reconciled with the Father. Those, who just accept Jesus as their savior and then go on to live their life as before, know nothing about the narrow gate. The narrow gate opens the door to the narrow way. The narrow way leads to Life, and few find it. Fewer still walk to the end of it.

From a standpoint of evangelism, knowledge of Kingdom life is essential. When we help people come to a decision to submit to the Lordship of Christ and then leave them to think that this is all there is, we do them a big disservice. The gate is not narrow and then gets less restrictive. All too often, we give the impression that the Christian life is not very different from being a non-Christian. The Christian Life is exciting. It is wonderful. It is an abundant life, Kingdom Life. However, it is also a narrow way of life. The gate is narrow and so is the way. It is Kingdom living. The pathway is chosen for us. We cannot decide to take another pathway and expect to get to the same destination.

The Christian Life is not just difficult at the beginning; it continues to be difficult. The Christian life is narrow from the beginning to the end. We are in error if we think that it starts narrow, hard, and difficult and then gets easier as we continue. The fight of faith goes right on through life to the end. There will be foes and enemies attacking you right until the very last minute. Because it is this way, *"There are few that find it"*.

There are things that we must leave outside the gate. We must leave behind the crowd, the life of worldliness. We must realize that in the Christian life, we become something exceptional and unusual. The Christian life is not very popular. Nevertheless, it is extraordinary, exceptional, strange, and it is different. It is a life of purity and holiness.

Paul, in his letters, has made it clear what this new life of Christ is to be like. In Colossians 3, he spells it out for us so that we will have no misunderstanding.

- *If therefore ye have been raised with the Christ, seek the things [which are] above, where the Christ is, sitting at [the] right hand of God: have your mind on the things [that are] above, not on the things [that are] on the earth; for ye have died, and your life is hid with the Christ in God. When the Christ is manifested who [is] our life, then shall ye also be manifested with him in glory.* (Vs. 1)

Paul tells us to *put to death*, in verse 4, the things that belonged to our old nature: *fornication, uncleanness, vile passions, evil lust, and unbridled desire, which is idolatry.* The people that commit these things will not inherit the Kingdom of God. It is because people are doing these things, that the wrath of God is coming.

He then goes on to say in verse 5, *put off or put away* things that must not a part of your new nature in Christ but are a part of your flesh; *wrath, anger, malice, blasphemy, vile language out of your mouth. Do not lie to one another, having put off the old man with his deeds.*

He is speaking to them and now to us, about the flesh. The things that have become a part of our daily living, those things that have become a part of our lifestyle, our culture and those things that are contrary to what He just had spoke; they cannot continue.

We need to leave "self" outside the gate. We must "put off" as Paul instructs us. They are not a part of Kingdom culture. There must be the working of the internal cross that we have already discussed and about which the Holy Spirit has been dealing with us if we are to enjoy the benefits of living in Christ's Kingdom.

Why is this so important? Verse 1 says we are raised with Christ in newness of life. We have Christ's life within us. We are to yield (surrender, give-up) our self-life in order that His life may live in us. We are to seek the things that are in the Kingdom of Heaven, where Christ sits on His throne next to His Father.

You can go and join a monastery but still have the way of the World within you. Living the way of the World and the life of the World in a different setting does not make you a Christian nor is it living the life of a Christian.

Jesus said 'the gate' leads to the narrow way and the way is hard. It is not an easy life. Someone was asked if the Christian life is difficult; he answered, "No, it is impossible".

It cannot be lived in the power of self. The standard set by Christ in the Sermon on the Mount is high. Thank God, that it is difficult. It is only a weak person, which wants it easy and wants to avoid the difficult.

The Christian Life is not an ordinary, everyday, run of the mill life. Anybody can do that; but the moment you want to do something unusual, or reach for the heights, you will find that there are not many trying to do the same.

The narrow life is a life of giving, and if truly lived, it will involve persecution. The World has always persecuted the man that pursues after righteousness. It is so now and it may be even more so in the last days before Christ's return. Let us then strengthen our inner man that we may be able to stand.

"Now the Spirit expressly says that in latter times some will depart from the faith, giving heed to deceiving spirits and doctrines of demons, speaking lies in hypocrisy, having their own conscience seared with a hot iron," (1 Tim. 4:1-3). Nevertheless, the promise is to us, as we follow this narrow way, we will enjoy the fellowship of His Sufferings.

The recommendation of the broad way is the ease with which it is walked and the great amount of people found along its path. It is as if they are flowing down stream, carried by the current. It is in the Broadway that the natural inclinations are not crossed and therefore, there is no interest in rowing upstream. The one disadvantage of this course of action is its end; it leads to destruction.

The end without Christ is a far worse end. Our Lord Himself spoke those parables about the foolish who did not count the cost—the man who started to put up a tower without counting the cost and so had to leave his building unfinished. The same is true of the king who went to fight another king, without assessing the strength of the enemy.

The Lord tells us to count the cost and to face what we have to do before we start. He shows us the whole of life. He has not merely come to save us from punishment and from hell; he has come to make us holy and to purify unto Himself a peculiar people, a family of sons who are zealous of good works.

The Judgment Seat of Christ

Notice again our diagram at the beginning of this Chapter. It shows that at the end of our journey there appears before us the Judgment Seat of Christ. Since we have pointed out that at the end of our days here on earth we shall stand at the Judgment Seat of Christ, a word about this great event is appropriate.

What might be interesting to point out is that everyone (the believer and unbeliever) will get to go to Heaven. Jeremiah 17:10 and 32:19 teach us that every member of the human race will be held accountable, *"according to his ways, according to the fruit of his doings."* The judgment of the unbelievers will be before the Great White Throne described in Revelation 20:15 but the judgment of the Believers will before the Judgment Seat of Christ.

Regarding the Believer; this is also foretold in 2 Corinthians 5:10-11, *"For we must all appear before the judgment seat of Christ, that each one may receive the things done in the body, according to what he has done, whether good or bad. Knowing, therefore, the terror of the Lord, we persuade men; but we are well known to God, and I also trust are well known in your consciences."* That "ALL believers will be judged" will show to all creation, the justice of our God.

Sometime between the resurrection of the dead along with the Rapture of the Church and the personal return of Christ at the Second Advent, every 'born again' believer will stand before the Judgment Seat of Christ. They will be judged for their works and receive their rewards. The Bible says we MUST appear; NO exceptions.

Our standing before the Judgment Seat of Christ instead of the Great White Throne was settled when we were 'born again'. Our sin was judged 'in Christ'. He took all our sin upon Himself and He took the entire penalty for our sin upon Himself as well.

The purpose of the judgment is to determine the value, the worthiness or the worthlessness of our works; those things we've done. Why is this so? Is it because we have been saved unto Good Works? Jesus will judge the motivation as well as the quality of our works.

'Good Works' are produced by walking in Fellowship with God and by being led or controlled by the Holy Spirit. Good Works are not produced by the power of man or within man but only by the power of God. The Fruit of the Spirit will be sought for among your good works. If there are no good works found or if they do not measure up to the standard, then your labor has been in vain. Do you remember the cursing of the Fig tree?

Believers will gain or lose rewards that are a result of their 'works'. We do not want to be ashamed or have to hang our head low when we stand before Christ. Who among us does not want to hear, *"Well done good and faithful servant"* when we approach Christ's judgment seat?

The rewards that are to be given out are not to bolster the servant's ego but to bring praise and glory to the King, who alone has made the good works possible. Good Works are the fruit of righteousness and they, therefore, will bring glory to the one who has been attributed to giving righteousness.

The rewards are revealed as crowns that we will cast at the feet of Jesus. There is the Crown of Life, The Crown of Righteousness, The Crown of Glory, and The Crown of Rejoicing.

God the Father is now calling out a people (The Church) that He might present them unto the Lord Jesus at the great marriage day of the Lamb. God is now preparing Christ's bride for this great celestial presentation. *"And to her was granted that she should be arrayed in fine linen, clean and white: for fine linen is the righteousness of saints."* WOW! What a day that will be!

The Bride will wear two garments that day.[i] The inner garment, that Christ gives us, and the outer garment, the weaving of our own good works. There is the inner garment of righteousness that comes to those that have received justification by faith. The inner garment is something that God bestows upon us when He washes our sins away and when we wash our robes (our souls) through the washing of regeneration and renewing of the Holy Spirit; He makes them white in the blood of the lamb.

There is also the outer garment of our own obedience to the mandates and commandments of our Lord. The outer garment is the deeds by which we do acts of faith to glorify the name of our Savior. The outer garment is that which we shall wear and it is woven by our own hands. It is made up of those things we have done that our Lord may be glorified.

This is the point now to take note of; Paul writes in First Corinthians 3:11-16 that ALL believers will stand before the Judgment Seat of Christ. As we stand before Christ in Heaven, our works will be tried as if by fire. If our works are wood, hay and stubble, they are burned; they are destroyed. If they are gold, silver, and precious stones; they abide as an adornment for the beautiful wedding garment we shall wear when we are presented to the lamb, *"...for his wife has made herself ready."*

Some of us will have on beautiful garments at the marriage. All the good things we have done in the name of Jesus and the works by which we have dedicated a holy life to the Savior; these will make up our garments that sparkle like the jewels of heaven and will be our rewards given at the precious hands of Jesus.

However, some of us are going to be practically naked, *"saved as by fire."* All their works will be burned up, all of them. Some of the things that these Christians do will be counted as nothing but worthless. These saints will come to the Marriage of the Lamb with nothing on but the inner garments. Is it any wonder then that Paul pleads with us, *"Therefore, my beloved brethren, be you steadfast, unmovable, always abounding in the work of the Lord, forasmuch as you know that your labor is not in vain in the Lord."* (1 Cor. 15:58).

The picture of you on your wedding day will be on display for all to see. What will you be wearing?

---

[i] C.A. Criswell, *Expository Sermons on Revelation*, preached while Senior Pastor at First Baptist Church, Dallas, TX, 1944-1994

Chapter Eighteen

Kingdom Sacraments

The Body Connection

Every Christian church provides its members or adherents the opportunity to take communion and involve themselves in Water Baptism. Communion and Water Baptism are what connect us to the Community of God in a physical sense. Water Baptism is a one-time act while participating in Communion is an ongoing act, whether it is daily, weekly or monthly.

Jesus stands in the present, with His arms stretched out connecting us to the past and to the future. In both of these Kingdom Sacraments He makes them both personal and corporate.

In Communion, Jesus reaches back to the Passover when the Children of Israel were delivered out of Egypt and then brought into a relationship with Almighty God. He reaches out into the future when He says, *"With fervent desire I have desired to eat this Passover with you before I suffer; for I say to you, I will no longer eat of it until it is fulfilled in the kingdom of God."* Luke 22:15-16

In Water Baptism He takes us back to the crossing of the Red Sea when the Children of Israel walked through the water and came out alive on the other side. He takes us into the future when the Apostle Paul said, *"Therefore we were buried with Him through baptism into death, that just as Christ was raised from the dead by the glory of the Father, even so we also should walk in newness of life"*. Rom 6:4

Communion

Every time we take Communion, we are affirming that we are remaining faithful to the covenant that we have entered into. As we stand in the midst of the congregation, we are making a statement; that we are in remembrance of the covenant made possible by the broken body and shed blood of Jesus Christ.

When we eat the broken bread, we are offering our lives as a living sacrifice. We shout that we are willing to die for our King, which is our reasonable service according to Paul. If this truth has not hit you, please stop right now and read *Fox's Book of Martyrs, Tortured for Christ* and Hebrews 11: 35-40.

When we drink from the cup, we are to lift it high for all to see because we are saying, "Long live the King". We proclaim to all that we are giving our allegiance, our loyalty, our hands to hold the sword and our feet to run to the battle in order that our King's kingdom shall be extended throughout the whole earth. Communion is very much personal, yet at the same time, it is also corporate. Communion is not done in a secret place; it is taken together with others that share the same love for Jesus Christ and the same allegiance to the King of glory. We are in relationship with one another.

Paul warns us that we are to examine ourselves before taking communion. We are looking for the lack of loyalty in our lives. It is this lack of loyalty, which results in our sin. If we look for sin only, it is like missing the forest because of seeing only the trees.

Jesus said, *"Not everyone who says to me, 'Lord, Lord,' will enter the kingdom of heaven, but only he who does the will of my Father who is in heaven. Many will say to me on that day, 'Lord, Lord, did we not prophesy in your name and in your name drive out demons and perform many miracles?' Then I will tell them plainly, 'I never knew you; Away from me, you evildoers!'"* (Matt. 7:21-23).

It is a time that we also allow the Holy Spirit to reveal our hidden sins that we might confess our sin and receive forgiveness. Nothing must be allowed to remain that will hinder our walk with the Lord. The term "Lord" should have special meaning for us because wherever it is written in the Bible it denotes ownership. We have been bought with a price, not silver or gold but with the precious blood of our LORD Jesus Christ. He is our King. Make the Kingdom connection. We are His and He is ours.

Water Baptism

As part of the Great Commission, Jesus commands us to go and make disciples and baptize the new converts. John's baptism was a baptism of repentance; a baptism that says that I have entered into a new way of thinking about the things that I've done. When we go under the water and come up, we are declaring that I once was a thief, adulterer, liar, whatever; but I have changed my thinking toward these things. I now hate these things that I once loved because they are an abomination to God, I have asked God for forgiveness and I am now a new creature in Christ.

I love what Paul said, *"Do you not know that the unrighteous will not inherit the kingdom of God? Do not be deceived. Neither fornicators, nor idolaters, nor adulterers, nor homosexuals, nor sodomites, nor thieves, nor* covetous, nor drunkards, nor revilers, nor extortioners will inherit the kingdom of God. *"And such were some of you. But you were washed, but you were sanctified, but you were justified in the name of the Lord Jesus and by the Spirit of our God."* (1 Cor. 6:9-11, emphasis added).

Something else changed for these new converts; they (you and I) are now citizens of the Kingdom of God. We have been translated from the kingdom of darkness into the Kingdom of the Son of God.

In any country that accepts immigrants, these immigrants are given very limited rights. They are given the right to work, drive a car, get an education and live anywhere in the country. However, they must register yearly and renew their green card, allowing them to work.

It is the expectation that each new immigrant would desire citizenship and therefore work toward the enrichment of his or her new country. Citizenship status, under social contract theory, carries with it both rights and responsibilities. "Active citizenship" is the philosophy that citizens should work towards the betterment of their community through economic participation, public service, volunteer work and other such efforts to improve life for all citizens.

Whatever their prior political or cultural position, it is no longer valid in the new country. If you came from Russia and were a communist, that position must be left outside the shores and the constitution of the new adopted country accepted. We must be reminded to keep looking ahead and not look back as Jesus said, *"No one, having put his hand to the plow, and looking back, is fit for the kingdom of God."* (Luke 9:62).

The parallel exists here for the Kingdom of God. The difference is that in becoming a citizen of the Kingdom does not involve a process; it is instantaneous. When we are "born again" we automatically become a citizen of the Kingdom. It is a birth right; Jesus said, "Unless one is "born again" one cannot enter the Kingdom of God".

Foreign nationals who wish to become citizens of the United States may do so through the naturalization process. Citizenship confers many advantages -- the right to vote, protection from the government, access to certain jobs and benefits, and the option to hold public office.

What does all this have to do with Water Baptism?

In Water Baptism, we identify with Christ in His life, death, burial and resurrection; that's personal. However, since it is public in nature, it also signifies a relationship with others that also have identified with Christ in the same manner; we have become members of the household of Faith.

In Water Baptism, there is a death side and a living side; a going down and a coming out of. We often talk about identification with Christ in Water Baptism because we haven't died physically. Yes, not physically but our death to sin is just as real as Christ dying on the Cross of Calvary. Let the words of Paul sink deep into your heart, *"What shall we say then? Shall we continue in sin that grace may abound? Certainly not! How shall we who died to sin live any longer in it? Or do you not know that as many of us as were baptized into Christ Jesus were baptized into His death"?* (Rom. 6:1-3).

We now live because Christ rose from the dead and has life. It is His life that He now freely gives to us who have also died. Paul said it so clearly, *"I have been crucified with Christ; it is no longer I who live, but Christ lives in me; and the life which I now live in the flesh I live by faith in the Son of God, who loved me and gave Himself for me".* (Gal. 2:20-21). This is so important because Christ's Kingdom is a kingdom of Righteousness.

In Romans, Paul admonishes us to walk a new way (a narrow way) when he says, *"Therefore we were buried with Him through baptism into death, that just as Christ was raised from the dead by the glory of the Father, even so we also should walk in newness of life".* (Rom. 6:4).

This new life of Christ means we are justified, which gives us a new position before God. This new position is citizenship in the Kingdom of God. Our citizenship in the Kingdom of God is a badge of highest honor and should be worn proudly. It should be seen by all, 365 days, as you live righteously in obedience to your new King.

Church attendance, going to Bible Studies, singing in the choir, being on the evangelism committee or editor of the church newsletter does not show that you now have met the standards or qualifications for citizenship. Only Water Baptism tells others in the Church that you are 'born again', and are going to live a righteous life without hesitation. You are proclaiming that you are now a citizen of the Kingdom of God.

Let us not cheapen the dynamic force of Water Baptism by just asking the candidates if they believe that Jesus is their Savior.

Chapter Nineteen

A New Season

Learning to live in the Supernatural

In the summer of 1973, shortly after I was 'born again', I had the privilege of attending a Bill Gothard Basic Youth Conflict Seminar. It was held at the Chicago Civic Center where about 5,000 attended. It was a wonderful 5-day event. For me, it was a time of transformation. I had been involved with a mainline church all my life but knew nothing of having a life changing experience. It was truly a Romans 12:1-2 moment in my life, a renewing of my mind by the Word of God. I thank God for that opportunity.

One thing that I was constantly hearing and reading from the Gothard material was, "we must relinquish our rights". We were servants therefore; we had no rights. God was in control and we must let Him have His way. It was said that everything that happened to us was a result of a loving God that was working out His purposes in our life. Gothard referenced the Apostle Paul calling himself a bond slave and Jesus saying that the greatest in the Kingdom is servant to all.

However, there was one thing that troubled me during the months that followed that seminar. Even with all that Jesus said about servant hood, I recalled that Jesus also said in John 15:15, *"No longer do I call you servants, for a servant does not know what his master is doing; but I have called you friends, for all things that I heard from My Father I have made known to you."*

Since I was developing my relationship with the Holy Spirit, I asked Him to reveal to me the fuller picture. This is where I believe the Church misses it. They are willing to be echoes, repeating what others have said, instead of being a voice, having received revelation for themselves.

As I read my Bible, it became clear that being 'born again' meant more than that I was part of God's family, it also meant I had become a Citizen of His Kingdom. If I believed this, then what was being revealed was a different mindset, a different Worldview from what I had received from Bill Gothard. If I was a Kingdom citizen, then I had rights that were awarded to me as a result of my new citizenship. Being 'Born Again' meant more than just going to heaven when I die.

If I was to accept this new premise of 'being a citizen of a Kingdom', then I must conclude that God's original purpose for His creation was to rule the visible world from the invisible. Because God had given Man a spirit, He could therefore communicate with Man and in effect, live in Man by planting his Word in his heart. Thus, in cooperation with Man, God would extend His heavenly Kingdom to Earth – the invisible ruling the visible, an invisible God ruling through a visible man.

Problem solved with a test

Trying to process these two conflicting mindsets was causing no little turmoil within me. I had to reach a conclusion. I was a King's Kid and a citizen of the Kingdom or I was not. I began reading and studying my Bible more. I read what others were saying on this extraordinarily important subject.

Then one day the test came; our family was driving back from Rochester, NY to Chicago where I was working as a Sales Engineer. We had gone to NY to pick up some bedroom furniture and mattresses. We had put them in the back of our pick-up truck, tied them down, put plastic over them and away we went. Of course, the plastic covering became useless as we drove 65 MPH down interstate 90 and 80.

As we were traveling through Indiana, a huge thunderstorm loomed in front of us. We could see the cars coming toward us with their windshield wipers still running. We could hear the plastic flapping in the wind and all we could think about was the mattresses getting soaked and ruined and what a mess that was going to be.

Although we were getting closer and closer to the rain, we knew not all was lost. We had remembered what we had studied in the Bible, what we had read in books like, "Like a Mighty wind" by Mel Torrey and others who had written stirring accounts of the miraculous power and love of God.

Bea got out our notes and our Bible and began feverishly looking up scriptures that would build our faith and then enable us to take dominion over the situation. Yes, take dominion, just as God had intended for man to do at the beginning and now made possible because Jesus had returned dominion back to those who were redeemed and "Born Again" into the family of God.

As our faith began to increase, we also began to speak it forth and as faith increased so did the peace that only Jesus can give. We knew, that we knew, that the rain would not come near our truck. We came closer and closer to the rain and as we did, the clouds began to part and just as we reached the rain – we could see the rain falling on both the right side and left side of our truck. The only water that hit our truck came from the splash as we drove through the puddles of water on the road. My Worldview was forever being changed.

We were convinced that God's Word was true but God was not done yet. He wanted to make sure this was settled in our heart. Six months later God revealed that He is still in the business of bringing forth dreams and visions. One night in January 1974, God gave to me a vision regarding foster children and a house. One year later, we moved into the very house that I saw in the vision with my family and two foster children. To tell of all the miracles that took place along the way would take to long. Nevertheless, it does bring us to the telling of another experience that deals with dominion and visions.

One year later, we moved to Mt Vernon, Ohio. God again had given to me a vision of our home. I went to see the local Real Estate man, Larry Lotz. I told Larry of the house that I had seen in the vision - in great detail. I knew he was a Believer because when I entered his office he was reading his Bible; one of those that has four translations. He closed his Bible and said, "Let's go". He took me straight to the house that I had described to him.

Let me tell you a little about Larry. Larry and his wife Caroline had been married for several years without having any children. When Caroline finally did get pregnant, they were the happiest people in the world. When Devin was born, however, their happiness soon turned to utter despair. When they brought Devin home from the hospital, all he did was cry and cry. After two days, they took that little bundle of joy back into the hospital only to discover that Devin was born without any Kidneys. That's right, No kidneys at all! They spent the night at his side with the doctors explaining everything about his condition.

Larry's story

The doctor told Larry and Caroline, "There is nothing anyone can do. The only thing left to do is to go home, get some sleep and ask the One above for help." His brother-in-law, who heard the doctor and feeling helpless himself, came over and said, "Why not ask God to heal him?" The lack of sleep, the heartbreak of Devin's condition and the sadness they saw in each other's face was just too much for them to handle. They left the hospital in tears and drove home.

Larry had gone to church in his younger years but at 18 he left and when he and Caroline got married, going to church was not part of their lifestyle. Larry himself admits that his life of drinking and being a part of the worldly scene did not lend itself to be thinking about God, no matter how bad things were for Devin. Certainly, that night, God did not seem very real to him.

When they got home, while still in the car, Caroline looked at Larry and said, "Larry let's give our lives to God and ask Him to heal Devin". They both cried out to God and told Him they would live only for Him and asked God to heal their son and give him kidneys so he could live.

The next day they went back to the hospital; there had been a change in Devin's condition. To make a very long story short, the doctor told him that something very unusual had happened. When they examined Devin again, they found that he did indeed have two very healthy kidneys. They could not explain it but there was no denying it and that Devin was healthy enough to go home. God heard their prayer that night and both Larry and Caroline have been living for their King ever since. When I met Devin, he was 5 or 6 years old; that was over 25 years ago.

Here is where we get back to the dominion part. Larry, now a Believer and OverComer, left the church of his family and sought out a Bible believing Church. He and Caroline began to grow in their faith and they read everything they could about this miracle working God that they now knew personally. They began to understand about the Kingdom of God and their place in it as citizens.

Then his faith was tested.

Larry and his family lived on a small farm in Fredericktown, Ohio. He was not a farmer but he did have some cows and chickens. One day during a storm, a funnel cloud formed just west of his property. He could see that it was coming his way and was about to touch down. Larry didn't have time to search out his Bible for Scriptures regarding Dominion; he didn't need to – he already had them in his heart. As the tornado touched down, he began to use his God given authority and commanded that tornado to bypass his property. He spoke to the storm just as Jesus had done and as I had done a few years earlier in Indiana.

People couldn't believe the story either when Larry told them, but there was no denying the truth when they came out and saw for themselves. The path of the twister ran right up to Larry's farm and then it mysteriously jumped over his property and came down again on the other side to continue on its way.

To enter a new 'season' with the Lord, your Faith will be tested. You know that your citizenship in the Kingdom of God will have real meaning for you and your family. Why not settle this now, once and for all. Commit your life and your Worldview into His hands.

Chapter Twenty

Response to Joni E. Tada

Healing Calmly Considered

On pages 27-28, we mentioned several assertions made by Joni regarding her healing and that of others. Because she has given herself to the Lord, He has promoted her to a position of influence. That position however, does not make her a spokesperson for God on the subject of healing. Unfortunately, her influence will keep many in their bed of affliction instead of praising God for His love and power. Allow me to address each one:

Joni: *"Does that mean "rise & walk" miracles are for everyone?"* The real question is, is there a need for a healing or a need for a miracle. Sickness and disease are the result of the rebellion in the Garden of Eden. Broken vertebrae, because of an accident, are something entirely different.

God created our bodies to heal naturally once the cause of the illness is removed. People go to doctors, get medicine and have operations to get rid of the cause so they can be healed. It is the same in the spiritual realm as it is in the natural realm.

If our condition is such that the body will not heal naturally, then what is needed is a miracle. A broken spinal column will not heal naturally, a torn rotator cuff will not heal naturally, and conditions such as MS, infantile paralysis, loss of eyesight and deafness are others that will not heal naturally. These all require a miracle, which is not found in the natural realm but only in the spiritual realm.

God has provided a remedy for every condition, whether it is healing for the sick or miracles for those in conditions like Joni's. God has provided His Word that will produce the faith required to bring forth either healing or a miracle.

This past Sunday, God gave me a perfect example to help picture what we have under discussion. A woman went up to the alter to pray. I was just standing at my seat worshipping the Lord. The Holy Spirit said to me, "Go and lay hands on her that she may get her miracle". I obeyed and went forward; just as I did, she got up from kneeling. I laid hands on her and she fell under the power of the Holy Spirit. I then put my hand on her jaw and prayed in the Spirit.

She came to me after the service and told me what was going on. She had been suffering for many years with a displaced lower jaw. It was made worst by her grinding her teeth at night. That day she was in much pain. When I put my hand on her jaw, the pain went away and her jaw was put back into its correct position. Praise the Lord.

In regards to sickness, faith in the finished work of Christ's atonement is required. In other words, Jesus' death on the cross not only made it possible to be forgiven but also to be healed. It comes in one big package called salvation. The Holy Spirit must make this truth real to you. It comes from revelation, not intellectual pursuit. Without accepting this truth, you can go no further. Your prayers will be full of doubt and unbelief; this will get you nothing but heartbreak.

Healing is for all Believers and you must settle it in your heart that God wants you personally to be whole, complete, healed. You must hear a Rhema word from God. A Rhema word is a word spoken directly to you from God. When you hear this Rhema word, faith rises up within you and you release it by proclamation because you know, that you know you are healed. Believers walk by faith not by sight.

Conditions, like that experienced by Joni, require a miracle but it is not a belief in Christ' atonement that is required. What is required is the operation of one of the nine gifts of the Spirit, the Workings of Miracles, by the person themselves or by another who is doing the ministering.

You can be healed and not know it right away. Healing usually takes time. Miracles, or acts of power, however, are seen immediately. However, some healings are manifested immediately and are therefore spoken of as a miracle.

For a broken vertebra, such as Joni experienced, to be restored to its original condition, faith in miracles must be present. God is still in the miracle business. Unfortunately, we have watered down miracles to such a great extent, it seems that anything out of the ordinary is considered a miracle. Such is not the case. Miracles are a supernatural event that has its start in heaven and reveals itself on earth.

A miracle requires Holy Spirit power. It requires a commitment from us to obey the commands given (an action to be taken) in order to receive. *"Take up your bed", "Go wash in the pool of Saloam", "rise up and walk"*, are commands given by Jesus and His Apostles; recognition and submission to His authority is required to receive your miracle. In the case stated above, it took my obedience to bring forth the miracle.

Joni: *"The Bible doesn't teach it and experience doesn't support it."* When a person does not receive what they pray for, they don't want to blame the lack of results on their lack of faith so they come up with another reason for defeat. Our 'reasons' for not receiving are just 'excuses' wrapped up in lies. This is hard to swallow but others can take just the opposite position and say the Bible does teach it and millions of people that were sick are now well.

Here is the point: We must not engage in any speculation as to why they are not healed. This is a very sensitive area and we do not want to discourage faith but to encourage faith in God.

However, let me address this issue. Just because people say they believe does not mean that, they have faith. Faith is the answer to everything. Faith comes from revelation not by study itself. Faith is given as a result of seeking God, not by trying to find the answer from pages in a book, even if it's the Bible.

Here is a bigger point: What we find in the church community today are people trying to persuade others to their point of view. They want to win an argument and thereby, feel superior about their knowledge of the Bible. I am not trying to win any argument but simply presenting truth that brings about wholeness to spirit, soul and body.

Joni: *"There are two conditions for answered prayer".* There are at least five conditions for answered prayer; not just the two that Joni mentioned. Joni has overlooked the last three conditions.

- Abide in Jesus – (John 15:7-8)
- Pray in accordance with the will of God – (1 John 5:14-45)
- Pray in the name of Jesus – (John 16:23)
- Ask in prayer, believing – (Matt. 21:22)
- Abide in the Word – (John 15:7)

Joni: *"... and that our requests be in line with God's will. Because God hasn't chosen to reveal every detail of his will to Christians, then we must leave our requests in His hands".* The problem is this; God has commanded us to pray according to the will of God. How can we pray according to the will of God and not know the will of God. The scripture says that, *"if we ask anything according to His will, he hears us: and if we know that he hears us, whatsoever we ask, we know that we have the petitions that we asked of Him".*

How could we trust God for anything if He doesn't let us know His will? Is this how you would treat your children, your loved ones? Do you keep them guessing as to what your will is? God does reveal his will to us by His Spirit. If we don't develop our fellowship with the Holy Spirit and sharpen our listening skills in order to hear His voice and promptings, we will come to our own conclusions. Joni's Worldview embraces Predeterminism. See page 51 in our book, "Greater Works Than These Shall You Do".

Joni: *"He will glorify Himself by our suffering."* There is nowhere in the Bible where God is glorified by the suffering of mankind. In fact, just the opposite is the case. It was when the sick were healed and the blind given back their sight that God was glorified. *"'Woman, you are loosed from your infirmity.' And He laid His hands on her, and immediately she was made straight, and **glorified God.**"* (Luke 13:12-13). *"And one of them, when he saw that he was healed, returned, and with a loud voice **glorified God**,* Luke 17:15-16, emphasis mine.

Now, if she means that through our suffering we are changed, as she was by devoting her life to God and learning to live with her situation, then is God glorified? Yes, others will see God at work within us but let us not say that God is limiting his glory because that is His Will.

To develop a good attitude toward her paralysis is not a miracle as she said. It is commendable, honorable, courageous, it is worthy of praise; but it is not a miracle. Hundreds of thousands of Christians around the world have fallen to a similar fate as Joni. These people, not having the same support system, money, and love from family and medical treatment have not been as victorious as she has. These have succumbed to bitterness, despair and have become burdensome to others instead of being productive in the Kingdom of God. Is this the work then of a sovereign God?

We are not called to be spiritual watchdogs or commentators on the faith or lack of faith regarding other believers. OverComers are called to present truths that WORK and change people's lives, God is not interested in our ability to win a theological argument; what He is interested in is for His people to trust Him and for us to take back what Satan has stolen. The truth will set others and ourselves FREE!

LEADERS ON FIRE

About the Author
Robert (Bob) Farrier

Robert Farrier, is an apostolic voice for today. He travels internationally proclaiming the gospel of the Kingdom of God and awakening God's people to the joy and reality of Kingdom Living. Through His Pastor's Conferences and books, he is exposing Christ's disciples to the adventure of being an OverComer.

For over 30 years, Robert has traveled overseas preaching on the streets to those who have never heard of the Redeeming Grace of the Lord Jesus Christ. Thousands have received Forgiveness, Healing, and Deliverance along with finding fulfillment in life as he proclaimed the Good News that the Kingdom of God has come.

Bob's recent activity has been in the nations of Haiti, Dominican Republic and Colombia, where he conducts Pastors Kingdom Conferences and is a sought after conference speaker. Bob also holds miracle rallies to reach the unsaved by showing the reality of God's power through Healings, Miracles, Signs and Wonders.

His heart is to reach out to pastors, that they might receive the revelation of the five-fold ministry and the message of the

Kingdom of God. His message imparts the revelation of the rule of Jesus Christ, the character and authority of its citizens and the culture of the kingdom that is to be revealed to the world. Churches in every nation are being changed as God's people are being transformed and empowered by the Holy Spirit.

Through Leaders on Fire, Bob is helping Pastors learn how to function in the grace given to them and walk in the supernatural. They, in turn, are helping God's people to find their giftedness that they too may fulfill their purpose and bring honor and glory to their king.

Robert is the author of two books, *NEW WINESKINS FOR NEW WINE, Turning followers of Jesus Christ into OverComers* and *"GREATER WORKS THEN THESE SHALL YOU DO", when your Passion for Christ finds expression; your life becomes an exhilarating adventure.*

Bob and his wife Bea have been married over 52 years. They reside in Loganville, GA.

You can contact Robert (Bob) at
leadersonfire@gmail.com

Bob is available for Kingdom Discovery Workshops and his books are available on the website, Createspace.com or on Amazon

Please check out Bob Farrier's website:
www.bobfarrier.com

Made in the USA
Charleston, SC
16 April 2015